New Poetries VI

an anthology
edited by Michael Schmidt and Helen Tookey

Nic Aubury
Vahni Capildeo
John Clegg
Joey Connolly
Brandon Courtney
Adam Crothers
Tom Docherty
Caoilinn Hughes
J. Kates
Eric Langley
Nyla Matuk
Duncan Montgomery
André Naffis-Sahely
Ben Rogers
Lesley Saunders
Claudine Toutoungi
David Troupes
Molly Vogel
Rebecca Watts
Judith Willson
Alex Wong

CARCANET

First published in Great Britain in 2015 by
Carcanet Press Limited
Alliance House
Cross Street
Manchester M2 7AQ

www.carcanet.co.uk

We welcome your comments on our publications
Write to us at info@carcanet.co.uk

A CIP catalogue record for this book is available from the British Library

ISBN 978 1 78410 037 7

The publisher acknowledges financial assistance from Arts Council England

Typeset by XL Publishing Services, Exmouth
Printed and bound in England by SRP Ltd, Exeter

Contents

Preface

'Suppose we made verses?' said Pécuchet.
'Yes, later. Let us occupy ourselves with prose first.'
Flaubert, Bouvard et Pécuchet

With this, the sixth *New Poetries*, the anthology series comes of age. It is twenty-one years since *New Poetries I* set the pattern, introducing new and relatively new writers, among them Sophie Hannah, Vona Groarke and Miles Champion, three poets so different that their art had to go into the plural. And plural it has remained. Twenty-one years, and twenty-one poets in this volume: some will go on to publish a collection with Carcanet (indeed one or two already have). Earlier anthologies have disclosed remarkable poets: beyond those already mentioned, Sinéad Morrissey, Patrick McGuinness and Matthew Welton (II); Caroline Bird, David Morley, Togara Muzanenhamo and Jane Yeh (III); Kei Miller (IV); and Tara Bergin, Oli Hazzard, Katharine Kilalea and William Letford (V) among many others.

More than half of the poets included in this book write rhymed and unrhymed sonnets. Shadow sonnets, ghost sonnets, sonnet shapes recur. Is this because as editors we are sonnet-haunted, sonnet-stalked? Or is there something about the sonnet form… we count thirty-three sonnets or near sonnets out of some 210 poems, and many longer and shorter poems reflect sonnet proportions, a 4/3 pattern. Sonnets ghost some of the prose poems. Were we to excavate backwards through the series we have a hunch that the sonnet has been a recurrent feature. As editors we do not have a particular sweet tooth for sonnets, but the poets whose work attracts us are concerned with form in ways that poets have experienced that concern for seven centuries, maintaining an oblique conversation with past and future and with one another, and all of them aspiring, if not to a place in heaven, at least to a share in Canto XXIV of the *Purgatorio* where Dante is welcomed as fulfilling and extending the promise of earlier poetries. There the *dolce stil novo* comes into being; here the reader can register how it renews and evolves.

Jorge Luis Borges wrote a poem called 'Un Poeta del Siglo XIII' ('A Poet of the Thirteenth Century'). This poet looks through the drafts of a poem. It is about to be the very first sonnet. He labours on a further draft, then pauses.

> Acaso le ha llegado
> del porvenir y de su horror sagrado
> un rumor de remotos ruiseñores.

To paraphrase, 'Perhaps he has sensed, radiating *from the future*, a rumour of far off nightingales'. Of things to come, even of impending clichés. The modern poet asks in the sonnet's sestet:

> ¿Habrá sentido que no estaba solo
> y que el arcáno, el increible Apolo
> le habia revelado un arquetipo,
>
> un ávido cristal que apresaría
> cuanto la noche cierra y abre el dia:
> dédalo, laberinto, enigma, Edipo?

> *(Had he detected he was not alone,*
> *that the cryptic, the inconceivable Apollo*
> *had disclosed to him an archetypal pattern,*
>
> *a greedy crystal that would detain,*
> *as night arrests day and then lets it go:*
> *Dedalus, labyrinth, the riddle, Laius's son.)*

For Borges the future weighs on this long-ago present, much as the past will come to do: in looking back, we see something aware of our gaze, returning it. This prolepsis, this analepsis, arrests the quill of the ur-sonneteer. It is a momentous little moment, a defining one. It's a moment many poets experience when they find a sonnet on their page. Those inherencies! Less a promise than an earnest. Once the sonnet is recognised by a labouring poet, not as a discovery but as a thing given by 'the inconceivable Apollo', once it is in language, as it came to be for Giacomo da Lentini in the thirteenth century Italian, it becomes part of something larger, in being successfully itself. This first sonnet, like those included in *New Poetries VI*, works with memory. Borges's poet, suspended between a classical *then* and a modern *now*, mediates. Our poets, too, mediate. A poet developing 'received forms' cannot but collaborate with the poems that came before and those that will come after. A sonnet never belongs exclusively to its author. When it has what Seamus Heaney calls wrists and ankles rather than hinges and joints, it is always new in its familiar, its familial movement. It pays its respects but has its own work to do.

A headline in the *Guardian* on 16 March 2015 proclaimed, '*Poems of the Decade* anthology swaps Keats for modern masters'. The word 'masters' is used loosely to describe the one hundred poets whose post-2000 poems have been commended for the Forward Prize. Keats suggested himself to the headline writer because the anthology has been adopted as an Edexcel A-level text in 400 schools and Tim Turnbull's 'Ode on a Grayson Perry Urn' was presented as displacing Keats's 'Ode on a Grecian Urn' in the curriculum. 'Hello! What's all this here? A kitschy vase', Turnbull begins. The third of his ode's four ten-line stanzas ends, 'Each girl is buff, each geezer toned and strong, / charged with pulsing juice which, even yet, / fills every pair of Calvins and each thong, / never to be deflated, given head / in crude games of chlamydia roulette.'

'Ode on a Grayson Perry Urn' may mark the distance between Keats's reflections and the contemporary world. Fair enough, though it devalues neither Keats nor his Ode, even in an age of compulsory 'relevance' in school texts. Daljit Nagra's 'Look We Have Coming to Dover!' does not quite displace its equally superannuated parent poem, Matthew Arnold's 'Dover Beach'. The poetry in *Poems of the Decade* 'will force a change in the way pupils view poetry,' says the *Guardian*. The subject-matter of poetry has been extended to include 'full-fat milk, Post-it notes, joy-riding, using guns'. This will be 'shocking [...] after dwelling on nightingales and Grecian urns'.

2014 marked the centenary of the beginning of the First World War and 2015 the fiftieth anniversary of the death of T. S. Eliot. The *Guardian* journalist is caught in a cliché, a narrow Romantic time-warp, unaware of Whitman's *Drum-Taps*, Rosenberg's 'Dead Man's Dump', *The Anathemata*, 'The Waste Land', the work of Auden, of Larkin and Plath, Ginsberg, Harrison and much else. Triumphalist ignorance sets out to 'challenge easy assumptions about what is and is not "literary"', portrays Keats as irrelevant, classical, conservative, disposable, and with him all the elitist, irrelevant clutter of past poetry and what it gives in terms of form, ear, living semantics. At last kids have 'poems for pleasure, not just for homework'—because the last thing a reader gets from Keats is pleasure. Time for some radical cultural cleansing. Enter *New Poetries VI* with its— sonnets...

Sonnets and other forms. The volume is characterised by a sensual, patient probing of and with form 'as jester or saboteur', as Adam Crothers, chief among the sonneteers, declares. There is a finding and forging of connections. There are a lot of birds here. And magic, the transforming kind that works now by charm, now by science. But before we become too formally fixated, consider the unaffected eroticism of Eric Langley's suspending repetitions, his syntax resisting closure, the tender, firm fingertips active on language as if trying to prove it skin, flesh and bone: and not a sonnet in sight. *New Poetries VI* is friendly to free verse when it is genuinely free of metre, or working powerfully within it, and doing the new things that modernism does so well, with hearing and with irony.

> The orthodontic meddling of language
> with the world, its snaggling malocclusions
> between a group of objects and their name

That's Joey Connolly: we can only imagine the pain he endured in the dentist's chair to reach that cacophony of images.

André Naffis-Sahely calls his poems 'episodes rescued, as Robert Lowell once put it, from "amnesia, ignorance and education"'. But is this right? He is not content with the formulation. How many poems are in fact remembering, how many invent memories? Is the rhetorical juxtaposition of ignorance and education more than rhetorical? Lowell without education? The romanticism of ignorance, poverty, the so-called 'natural man' have sell-by dates. Nyla Matuk evokes, in another context of escape from what we are, a 'bourgeois notion masquerading / as real life.' Her sea-shells are occupied by monsters and molluscs: she has managed to use poetry as a way of unknowing herself. When Brandon Courtney writes 'Reality, in plain language, is paramount in my work', he has defined how difficult it is to arrive at that plainness, how much has to be discarded on the way.

> My father says the war changed me
> from a killer to a pacifist; I refuse
>
> to fillet the fish he pulls from the lake.
> I refuse to slip the blade between gills,
>
> fold back their pearlescent scales,
> cut away what little meat their bodies
>
> offer.

One might think that his unique selling point is his subject matter: he is a war poet and has been in the thick of action. But though the adjective comes first in 'war poet', the noun element is 'poet', and that is what went to war, and what came home, wrestling the experience into language and form. Subject matter is never enough, unless we want our poets to be journalists. As C. H. Sisson wrote of Wilfred Owen, the poetry is not in the pity, but in the poetry.

Each of these poets seems to have an almost epithetic image: a seashell, say, or teeth, or fingertips, foreign cities, wind, alleys, gardens, a fascination with the spaces of others – other times, other genders. We as editors relish this variety and the variety of tones. There is a good deal of laughter in this book, including poems that might be described as light verse – which deserves its equal welcome at the high table, as it always has. There is also ambitious experiment, in the formal exigencies and nuancing of syntax in the vivid elaborations of Alex Wong's poetry and in the unrestrained invention and discovery of Vahni Capildeo's.

In February 1955, anticipating the publication of his sequence *The Nightfishing*, the Scottish poet W. S. Graham wrote: 'With all its mistakes and blemishes I think it is a knit object, an obstacle of communication, if you like, which has to be climbed over or gone round but not walked through. I think it just might make its wee disturbance in the language.' If as editors we were to look for communal ground among the works here, Graham's notion of a poem as an object made of words, that creates a 'disturbance' in the language, might provide a starting point. The poets in *New Poetries VI* share a consciousness of the English language – coloured by place, by other languages, but nonetheless a common tongue for the North American, British, Trinidadian, Antipodean – as their medium. They explore it with old and new-made tools, they push and prod, they bring other languages and times to bear upon it. It sings and also clashes with itself, against itself.

And Graham's phrase 'an obstacle of communication' resonates: there is a contrariety about the very act of writing poetry, fixing something in a language which often imitates the ephemeral intimacy of speech, imposing measure on it, containing and rhyming it. Graham develops the idea of 'obstacle': the poem has to be 'climbed over' or 'gone round'. Basil Bunting spoke of the *Cantos* as the Alps that had to be crossed. On a smaller scale, our obstacles cannot be simply 'walked through'. Poetry is not communication in the usual sense of the word, imparting information. Nor is it mere opacity, indirection, slant. There is little place in poetry for that kind of deliberated obscurity, confusing thickness with depth. For Graham the solidity of the poem is like the solidity of a lighthouse, a point of permanence, a mark, a warning, a welcome. He expects the reader to see and hear the poem, to *experience* it. Visitors to Graham's cottage at Madron, Cornwall, were sometimes invited, almost before they were through the door, to read one of his poems aloud. They were judged on the performance and either invited in for a cup of tea or Teachers, or told that the poet was not at home. The poem was a threshold, a word he used in the title of another collection.

Brandon Courtney, in the note to his poems, stresses that he wants his poems to be accessible to a reader. He doesn't 'strive to create new images' because the images with which life has confronted him are real enough. Yet in the first of his poems here, 'Beforelife', the poet visualises himself before birth, 'asleep in an abandoned skiff, / just one among hundreds / in a boneyard / of boats'. There are some things poets cannot do without, however demanding their experience, however predictive the language.

As editors we want this to be an anthology of durable disturbances written in a variety of Englishes, relating to a range of landscapes and timescapes. Disturbance can be resistance, and it seems to us that poetry by its very nature — focusing language, holding it up, in both senses, and letting it go, in both senses — is resistance of an invigorating kind. Clichés and commonplaces are laid bare and, if they are not consciously deployed and ironised, they damage the poem, unmake the disturbance. Alert and self-conscious language need not appear as such to the reader, and in an achieved poem its radical awareness is not what readers perceive but what they experience. It is only afterwards, returning, that they begin to explore the mechanism.

Judith Willson

I am fascinated by the ways in which silence and absence are not voids but textures; by the insistent, unstable presence of the past, and by the languages which transform how we understand these things.

I write slowly and revise repeatedly, listening for the point at which ideas cohere into shape and rhythm and the poem finds its direction. If this works, I know something new when I have finished.

I have adapted several details in 'Some favourable effects on bird life…' from E.M. Nicholson's *Birds and Men* (1951). Nicholson was an ornithologist, and a civil servant during the Second World War. The italicised lines in stanzas 1, 3 and 4, and the last line of the poem, are direct quotations. 'The alchemy of circumstance…' takes its title from Tacita Dean's description of photography in her *Analogue: Drawings 1991–2006*. Phrases in brackets and italics appear in Dean's artwork *Blind Pan*; some are themselves from *Oedipus at Colonus*.

Noctilucent

We cross the garden: slant sun, slack tide of shadow.
He is remembering woods below San Pietro, the ragged end of a war.
Soldier and red-cloaked shepherd on the road,
the old man stilling his dog, waiting in the white road.
He watches now: his stumble down, wading knee-deep
through tangled nets of dazzle, spills of shade,
to the soft chalk curve between the trees,
the red cloak burned in his eyes. His hand, unsure.

He says, *If a person walking raises his hand*
he sees the shadow of each finger doubled.

Trees slide down to lap us, attentive to our solitudes,
until the hollow dark is filled with memory of light –
fluorescence, phosphor glow, poppies' slow burn;
ghostlights to guide our double-going.

All this

This is where it all comes home to us, in the fetch of light
crossing the mirror line and only a bank of concrete blocks

grounds us here in the level give and take of the estuary now
the machinery miles down between Stavanger and Bergen

begins to heave the whole weight of the sea round; long rigs churn
back over the *Blessing of Burntisland*, heap into the firth

in a shining skim that hauls its undertow of sky across the silt
buckling the mudflats open; we are dissolved in this now

our edges bloom underwater and the sanderling livewire
at the lick of foam sheer away in scuds of grey-white

white-grey, wheel back, a shower coming in off the sea.
All this. And sea urchins, *Echinocardium*, blown from the surf

like bubbles of bone, the amazed *O* of all we could lose.
Our weightless luck. Our brittle, spiky hearts.

Hushings

hushing: to silence; to wash out mineral deposits by releasing a torrent of water

Clough

Up on the tilt where the moor begins its slide into Lancashire
and the village shrinks back at the sour peat out past the turbines
we're trying to make sense of what isn't here:
a clean sweep of mountain wasted sheer into wind,
glaciers that snouted down from the north in a roar of rubble and sinkholes,
burst open, sluicing green meltwater, drifted off into hag fleece,
goits and headraces, limekilns, the yellow drench of their smoke.
There's a whole phantom moor in this washed-out clough
and we're feeling our way by echo location
towards a hurly of diggers and carters, stokers, women hefting picks.
Every winter the light falls more thickly, layer upon layer.
The hushings are deepening by one millimetre a year.

Ore

There are things we remember only because of their absence,
like a word I need for the light that blows in from the west
after rain, or the hollow house in a field of bleached grass
we walked to one hot afternoon – and now we've both lost the path back
you think I've imagined the moment we pushed open the door
onto summers of butterflies faded and heaped like old letters,
their dry sift over the floor, their tiny stir in the draught.
My father once told me a secret he'd learned as a child:

the exact spot on the pavement where, if you stood very still,
you could hear the river running beneath the street –
a trap opening onto something implacable that would always be waiting.
He remembered that all his life, but not where to stand.

Snow

after Salvatore Quasimodo, 'Neve'

Evening gathers into itself the earth and all its dear ones:
gaunt men pulling military greatcoats round their narrow bodies,
women wrung dry with crying. It dissolves trees into wind;
it hollows us out to starved shadows dragging our heels
over the fields of a planet lit by snow-shine.
It gives us to our dead. We do not howl into the dark
as we should. We do not beat our fists against the iron-black rim
of this white sphere where our people lie buried around us.
We give them the angry pulse in our foreheads, our heartbeats.
They take the shape of breath from our mouths. We walk in silence,
and in silence snow and night enfold us all, so tenderly. So tenderly.

Some favourable effects on bird life of the bombardment of our cities

Wrynecks were constantly heard around British Headquarters
during discussions of aerodromes. Swallows looped over the lake.
I watched the salients of their swerves, scribbled on a memo
The destruction of the human population
is no longer such a remote contingency as it used to seem.

There's a blackbird and a throstle sing on every green tree

I never discuss Allocation of Tonnage or movements of ships
outside this room. I trace the perfected migrations of swifts,
flight patterns of lapwing, scan winter skies for starlings, wait
for the rolling thrum of their sideslip over ministry buildings.
I follow dancing parties of goldfinches on frivolous excursions.

and the larks sing so melodious, sing so melodious

I do not entirely trust the Civil Service. Shortages of bacon and milk
may have caused a curious habit newly observed in bluetits –
papers shredded, notices ripped. *Bombing, favourable effects of,*
I slot into the card index, between *Birmingham* and *Bradford*.
Starlings are roosting now among the anti-aircraft guns.

and the larks sing so melodious at the break of the day

I write *The disappearance of the human race from these islands*
would perhaps most inconvenience the lesser whitethroat.
A blackbird clamours brazen, jubilant, jubilant,
fireweed and cinders, a shattered hedge.
I shall persist in calling the song thrush a throstle.

Amateur magician

Learn these tricks for an amusement, but do not carry them into your everyday life.
— J. Theobald, *The Amateur Magician*

I studied how to cut the Princess of Thebes into nine pieces
and pluck the Lady of Karnac to hover at my fingertips
over a pit of flames. They'd have danced back every time,
those flexuous girls, to catch the paper bouquets
I'd whisk from my gloves.

And then, Swallowing the Needle, the Knife through the Heart –
the trick is to leave no visible traces. Palm up palm down
here's a coin in your ear, here's your purse in my hand
before you knew it had gone. Your ear-ring?
Watch me cut open this apple.

What followed came easy: the Riffle Shuffle, the Faro Shuffle,
the snap and fan of Lost Queens descending a staircase again, again,
all the false cuts, false dealing, the Criss Cross, the Switch.
I mastered the Ambitious Card; fumbled the Finger Break.
It would always be Double or Nothing.

And look, there's nothing between my hands, nothing up my sleeves –
only a length of silk ribbon I'll walk through, without a cut or a knot.
It's Expansion of Texture, that trick that makes nothing appear.
It's my gift.
I've left you my Vanishing Card.

The alchemy of circumstance and chemistry
in five photographs
Tacita Dean's *Blind Pan*

[Exile, no sun]

This is a photograph of twenty years. There are no people
in it, and no shadows. He carries this famine
on his back; he carries his country in his mouth
and it has no word in it for *home*, no proverb of forgetting.

[Antigone leading, dark clouds]

Walking under rain. *Who was your father?* Gunfire in villages,
dogs at the gates. What does her voice look like?
Like the weight of her coat. Like bread. Like *Take my hand,
walk in my footsteps.* No. *Who was your father?* Like rain.

[Furies, 'your steps are dark']

Forests run howling for water; air shredded, wingbeats.
She cannot look into the burning, curls under herself
as if she were unborn. *Walk in my footsteps.* Her hand.
He leads her over the border, into dark, out of sight.

[Colonus, just out of frame]

Halting, lame. Halt where a spring overflowing a basin
returns his face to him in silver and sunlight slipping over the brim
through wet, open hands, into black earth. He sees the place
when he knows it. No one can look direct into the sun.

[Light. End here]

It begins, *no way back*, in a dark room, something taking
the imprint of light. In this photograph are constellations,
musics, scribbled maps, our chancy travel across peopled time,
and there is no exposure long enough to make this visible.

James Turrell's *Deer Shelter Skyspace*, Yorkshire Sculpture Park

Temple, lake, deer shelter triangulate arcadia's vanishing point.
Leaves skitter in the empty summerhouse; beyond the sliding water
shadows herd beneath the arches of the deer shelter.

★

Walk into a concrete silo open to the sky.
There's nothing to see here.
What does nothing look like?

Flying over the curve of the Painted Desert, air opening like water,
barrel-rolling over fathomless sky in Pyramid Lake; farm lights at night
                                                    far-flung as stars.
At dawn, the hangar shining: a memory of sunlight on a wall.

*

7.30am: mussel shell; split of gold; skirl lifting and spilling,
1pm: ragged pennants; vapour swags; sting of rinsed shorelines,
5pm: damson stain; smoke feathers; ink.

That this is nothing – how do we live with this?
We stare like deer into the event of light.

The years before

That time my grandmother went to the sixpenny hop
in the years before they became the years before
Tom Baxter and Rabbity Dixon played through the roiling night
of longways and hands across down the middle back again and
turn and *K-K-K-Katy* and *Haste to the Wedding*

     and oh how

Tom could play the birds out of the trees with that old concertina
pouncing and bucking high jinking over the honk and growl
of what moved in the forest at the edge of the tune
Rabbity sharp and quick as his traps to snare the beat
sending the tambourine's silver starlings whorling

     over and over

towards a room she walked into one afternoon
when Will ran into the kitchen *come down to the shop*
you must come and see this there's a man here says he's a
and there among boxes of collars and gloves resting palm to palm
the day quietly folding its hours away she shook hands with a lion tamer

and heard again

all that wild blaze reeling and swooping
heel and toe stamp turn about and
Goodnight Ladies and oh *The Girl I Left Behind Me*
somewhere out in the forest rough music rising
in the year that was becoming the year before

Watching a nineteenth-century film
in the twenty-first century

Adolphe, Mrs Whitely and Harriet wait in the garden
still in an angle of sunlight
that will never fall across the bay window
or slice the mottle of summer-weighted shade.

They take four steps to turn into the shadows
at the edge of their afternoon;
four steps wheeling past us – skirts swinging, coats flapping –
a breath's length away as we watch in their dark.

Their bodies are a shower of particle-scatter,
their footfall a trick of snapshooting time.
They flicker to the edge of the frame at twelve frames a second
for two seconds for ever
through a speckle and grain of sound too distant to reach us:
Adolphe counting their steps – and turn –

a neighbour's shout, a laugh, a road beyond the hedge spooling out, out
into the smash and roar of the world that's falling towards us.

In the jagged months

In the jagged months when you lost even lost
and knew it, you gave up arguments and grievance –
those intricate machines you had built for years,
their ratchets kept oiled and sharp to run sweet –
and broke glass. Your hand was a wrecking bar
smashing ice on a pond, you splintered yourself open
to haul down through a mulch of black leaves for what lay
in the sump of winter's slow bruising.
You had seen them, bent under four o'clock dark
throwing your box in the pond, the box that held your streets,
your tools, the white leaves of your books, your days of the Arno –
days when green branches swaying upside-down in a pool
rose like a promise through the pliant skin of water
which opened to your hand, and was whole again.

Eric Langley

I am trying to pay attention.

Attempting to tenderly attend.

In writing these poems, I wanted to take the time to become fully attentive to a chosen word's extended meaning until perhaps, by playing on its sense and sound, and enjoying its possibilities, I could somehow tenderise each word, release its etymological potential, make it more malleable through this application of my tender attentions. Hopefully, as the connective tissues of sense get tested, heated past 55°C through the quick frictions of rhyme, the word's semantic fibres, its collagens and collocations, start to loosen and get tastier. Sense extends; new meanings are tendered up: poetry becomes tenderness.

And to be attentive is, as the word's origin suggests, to stretch out (*tendĕre*), to go beyond one's confines: so these are intended as tender poems, stretching across interims, sending out words into the spaces between people, trying to connect. They are a bit bruised in their encounters, often a bit wayward, and always feeling tender: but as Judith Butler admits, 'one does not always stay intact. [...] Let's face it. We're undone by each other. And if we're not, we're missing something.'

Of Those From the Ships

Ptolemaeus the king of Egypt was so eager to collect a library, that he ordered the books of everyone who sailed there to be brought to him. The books were then copied into new manuscripts. He gave the new copy to the owners [...] but he put the original copy in the library with the inscription 'of those from the ships.'

– Galen

So you can come along and you can scan it:
come along the docks, as are your curious customs,
and you can move among my spread
among my freight my cargo.
And you should catch a draft to drift
to drift from crate my love to crate
my love through freight my lovely argosy.

So you can leaf your dusty tips through wheat and chaff
and riffle out each inky index
through all the silken slough
of all my gaudy textiles.
Flick through it, resort it, recall it
to recount and to your count enlist
my disembarked, my unencrypted holdings.

And so, ascribe each part, just so,
inscribe each piece, just so,
describe each Hippocrene flask, just so,
each cask, just so: of all my all content.
To each a place in place to place
in your exact accountant call
of row by rolling row anatomies.

Now as you go, steady
my dizzying inventories, steady
my whole to holed in hold and steady as you go.
Until amongst the richer sort, my finer stuff,
my love, my weft, my warp, my woof, my loom,
you come across, you chance upon
my books, my textured library.

Like Antony, enlisting scrolls for Egypt,
I've weighed up with ranks of primed romance,
rows of charged letters, waxed flattery.
Please read them quick; respond at length but
on the instant, as each squeezed line tips
tight up on the grazed edge, squeaks 'come!'
and soft speaking means the softly same.

Pinched, each plundered volume plumbs
your depths of cheek of face of front.
The bitter gall of it, from row to row
shelf to shelf and decimal point to point.
You and your low-toned underlings, *sotto voce*,
unstack, stack up, pack up and off
with those, all those from my ships.

Your tough customs, your officious vandals,
all horn-rimmed reading glasses
all hob-nailed boots spectacular
along my aisles, through my stacks,
scrawling down my gang-planks.
So silence please. And no talk back to back
to no recourse to no redress to silence please.

You rogue librarian, filling packing cases;
you rough justice, packing shipping crates;
you vile bibliophile, stealing a borrow;
you unrepentant lovely lender.
Fingered, found red-handed
shameless-faced, each fly defaced:
of those – you wrote *– from the ships.*

You with your hollow whispers
of silenced, pleased apology,
towing away my textures
of those from the ships.
You book thieves pirates book robbers;
you book thieves collectors borrowers lovers
of those from the ships.

Of course, I knew your Alexandrian law.
I knew you'd come, and knew you'd take them.
Of course, I brought along my best materials –
first editions, originals, manuscripts –
and must have hoped you'd steal them.
This is the hope, of course off course,
of all those from such a stricken ship

of all those from the ships.

Glanced

I

You lovely looker on and by and by and.
One-eyed Cupid, locked, cocks, and shot

Zeno's arrow at Zeuxis' grapes.
Shaft straight. The pointed

parabola arced its homeward hoops on its
wondering way through loop and loop

towards my eye's apple; its
projectory now arches down to heel to hit

or miss, may kiss the head or glance off
on bow bend or twisted thread.

My flighted hope: that bird cracks glass, and tumblers
beakers breaks on painted grapes

on picture plane or bounce back
deflected, as mote on float

reflected. Map the rebound cause
I am sore astound and all amazed,

while flecks dart and seeds quiver
quiver while the heavy freighted interim

divides
by half by half by half.

Split hairs or ends or seconds now sub-divide
by half and half, as hare's breath

on tortoise's collar falls and arrow
tip elbows each atom aside

to side or sneaks contracted
kiss, a peak, a contact passing

charge in the charge in the change
from Z to thee kinetic.

II

Keep lovely looking on and over
looking keep looking till

your lead tip punctures what, back then, was
walnut, poppy, hemp, pine and olive; then

a resinous gloss, of Paris Green,
of arsenic, of mercuric sulphide;

then, later, *oglio cotto*, honeyed
lead oxide; then beeswax;

now, bladder-pod, ironweed, calendula,
sandmat, in slow drying strata

of alpha-linolenic, brittle as it brakes,
of crisp linoleic, of still wet oleic acid, still wet.

Then warp canvas warped.
Then wall.

III

So keep on lovely looking on,
no overlook, from then to now, as now

the paste-board splits
and peck hits home and

dry eye and true to touch
and each grape breaks and

tortoise tumbles down hap with hare
and tip touches now, and now, and when

and then just so, soothed through
freeze frame and bending glass,

each hot pigment shot and then
and then, keep lovely looking till.

So glancing blown by,
so palpably hit away, so

keep so lovely looking still
keep lovely looking till

until each hungry bird
has flown and had his fill.

Tact

By the privy entries of the eare,
words sappe downe
into the heart, and,
with gunshotte of affection,
gaule the mind,
where reason and virtue
should rule the roste.

I. FIRST REPETITION

Immediately so
and so as palm to palm
do our kind contracts kiss.
Immediately to
intergraft in such soft contacts,
tact to tact
skinful of our fuss
of warm brushed haptic.
Immediately by
hap to hap contracted
to our eyes' kiss.
Unmediate.

II. SECOND REPETITION

If I could lap myself
up tight so tight to
you, we (you and I)
could crush out and.
If I could lap us
tight so to we you I
would crush out
first person
personal.
If lap us
tight we
crush.

III. THIRD REPETITION

Need no postman for
each hap riposte; need
no interim parcel
force; need no parole patrol;
no punctuating drum;
nor nurse; nor Friar Peter;
need no re-prefix as we fine flex
ply taut cord petition, storing places
membering port to post
signed to it. Turn and turned again,
bound to the turn and turn.
Nobody interfering, over here.

IV. FOURTH REPETITION

To touch: to move or grieve; to
come; to deceive;
to quip; to taunt; to take up; to
write; to speak,
or mention a thing.

V. FIFTH REPETITION

To be sent back
I step back
make room back up
push space to stare
slot intervals interim
a mediating as we
throw out into a busy medium.
The bounce between us
links out lovely chain
causal interactions hot
on heels, lagging cause to
overlapped event, coat over coat
laid out and over. Without the

gap, perhaps we can't
get intimate.
You snap distinct only
on the far side of
a mediating tumble.

VI. FINAL REPETITION

And are the ethics of adoration that
I stand far back enough to stare?
Listening intently behind the closed door
to you to you as you.

Rete mirabile

So now the restless man awakes
out beyond the harbour wall
plunged by wake washed conduit
bathed interlaced in channels
involved among their flow and spread
of cadent fall and fret and runnel
of giddy net of saturated space.

> [*I wake unfolded out*
> *over twenty-one square foot of deck*
> *each cutaneous square inch*
> *a thousand-fold of nerve*
> *still sensible to a long extended press;*
> *your still, your lucid touch prolonged*
> *through corneum, lucidum, basale*]

Go give the care-held keel a kick;
set rank to signal breakers now.
Dig the heel to catch careen on roll
along about the reel the stagger
tossed and scattered. Torn to tatters.
'I'm far away out here', I said.
Inside your dazzling influences.

[*You sloughed clean through*
thirty dead cell layers
– the basal lamina
insular epiderm –
imprinting tense connection
deep in the elastic heart
through reticule and papillæ]

I am all out along electric clamour,
among swan's song translated
into a swan's cry, a swan's blare,
in the dull distort of gull music
(but 'lah-di-dah', is all they say)
and still my mews' song sounds
loud around the gulls' mewling.

[*depth projected through*
scarf skin gloss skin
to kiss off this true-skin.
Mine corium my derma:
you inscribed upon the underside
with careful impress:
all mine from the ships]

And so caught out in stormy weather
the grand mystery of flux & reflux,
the flowing and ebbing of the sea
my mind gets blown by aggregate emotion
by vigorous simpathetical connexions.
Streams, it seems, do entwine with streams.
And lakes do twist with lakes.

[Touché, *you touched the nerve net,*
tocca, *hit homing over canal and cleft*
along the plate and groove through glue
to toc *down on the synapse, axons, radials:*
those inside dazzling influences
those mesenteric sympathetic plagues *from*
fibres felt down dear, down down in the gut]

Nothing to say about my self
as simply complete:
or intermingled admixture.
Nothing of concrete self to say
the one way or the other.
So much of me was in the interim,
and that much left around your library.

[*Go open your eardrum. Obey, and be attentive.*
Tease out integrity along this feeling line.
Impact me out, redound me: beat
tender integers, and make me unintact.
Down me soundly each tendon unbound me
wholly; fractional; entirely; touched till taut.
Go list, lean in: I barely am intact. I barely am.]

I turn the ear. *Ahem.* Hope for feedback.
Tacit *ishin-denshin*, dear System I.
I turn the ear. Catch only tenor,
sound of stretching oars extending,
the fed-back beat, the stroke, beat, stroke;
catch curlew's calls through spindrift,
crying, something, barely understood. *Amen.*

She Picked Out Puncture

We view the rock-paved highways worn by many feet.
We see how wearing-down
has minished them.

She picked out puncture
in the curve of worn stone steps,
that snagged the scene

and caught her with an attented hook and tug:
a soothed snag.
It took red dust, lucid air,

red air, parched grass, and lifted
all of them, to pinch their tuck, to nick
from guidebook and touch-up the map.

A snap, an instant capture.
A really represented. A naturalish truth
beyond the studious. Piercing glass.

Taut, the swerve and concave bevel
gave her stumble, brought her up short,
said 'what is' and then 'what was' and 'what has ceased to be'.

A tension from inclined tread under foot fall
lent something more than scenic
to *toppled masonry and ponderous stone.*

A cut, not cut but smoothed away
by punctual coincidence of foot and stone,
by accident of contact over time,

and fall of feet and feet and level rain
which flows and flows in mighty bend reverberate.
A shelled out bruise, a bay,

a thumbed out dip that gives each step
its line, its mine,
its distinct decline.

And caught, now, among these declinations, punctuations –
the spatial grammar of lateral column, horizontal wall –
she is what happens, what befalls.

And so, the hedging air is fetched
to forum
just to gaze on her.

And I know she pushed the groove
in with her heel, and felt it out
and lent it weight

(although I wasn't with her
and others were).
Just light hair, light shade, and cool concaved stone.

My mind is not deceived how dark it is, but
    large hope
hath strook through my heart.

And I sat dumb stunned in a market place
and felt the vertigo of the earthbound
among the atoms' fall.

For lightnings pass through iron white-dazzles
rocks burn with exhalations fierce burst asunder
tottering in heat

'It is,' she said, 'what you wouldn't notice
unless you didn't look
that cuts across this drift and tumble'.

And I wish I was with you
when you glanced
and glance it.

And my hedging thought is fetched
to forum
to chance on you.

Vaucanson's Duck

Monsieur Vaucanson, well-known for his automatic machines,
Has now come to this city to share with the Académie his plan.

Vaucanson's duck –
with fragile hoops
unplumed, unflighted
of quill, of spine, *rachis*;
with plated eye
caught all up.
all caught up

with wire sprung neck,
declining;
by metallic fishbarb
with panelled face
unsighted – sits still,
His brittle ankle
in massive mechanism.

But soon, mesdames messieurs,
the lack of wings
each steel cog tooth
in bolted pig-iron ironframe,
and trip quick animation
sprung to lifelike.
its bill and beak,
this plucked duck, with luck,

beneath
each wheel on massy wheel
– of face and pitch –
will rachette up
in my automate,
With quack and flap,
its neb and tuck,
will up and up.

Motivation, emotion, move me.
and up and into sinew
Rhythmic lurches
artful arch articulate.
moves, moved by
And hefted to its shifts,
it pumps unfeathered wings,
from webbed roots,

Wind up
undulated strives.
unbind to wind out across
Skeletal delicacy
cranked energia.
its punctual catches,
pulled up
pneumatic plumps

chest puffed rebuffs
And look, he's up away
with the breeze
round coil electric
Catches, catches the drift.
Lucky strokes,
tucks swerve round accident
out of frame,

the big wind up and up.
pneumatic
that winds its currents
animate.
so swerves.
beat, stroke,
and off,
unbuckled.

Vaucanson can't believe his duck,
and can't account its indirections;
it flits our expectations, it defies prediction
in wilful predilection perverse inclination
inclined, clined, declines decline
branch from root misled, sent sideways,
lull, jolt, shoot out in semantic skid and pull,
spelling out canards in weasel limbed whales.

He cuts across clouds wetting his wings
on the rain drops they hold and disrupting
a turbulent shower a cumulus. His rupture
sends spray precipitous cascades fall
as he writes his passage diagonal
spinning in his scripted wake.
Leaves Vaucanson as a
startled I.

Adam Crothers

There's a Richard Herring stand-up routine in which two characters, burning to death, react to the failure of their punchline by aggressively deconstructing first their status as fictions and then their author's performance and career. I doubt I quite achieve this ideal in my writing; but I value the principle that a poem is a breathing thing with no particular responsibility to outward virtue or to making its poet look delightful. I'm interested in form as jester or saboteur, in irony as honesty, in the transcendent moment as desirable but doubtful, and in the poem that allows itself to be soundtracked, sidetracked, by other texts (superior poems; country songs; black metal) and alters accordingly its negotiation tactics or interrogation methods. While I have some enthusiasms in common with the speakers of these poems, I'm not sure we would all get along.

A Fit Against

The left hand knows what the right rear leg wants.
The centaur's cento splices *Black Beauty* and *Frankenstein*.
He likes to correct people, tells them Beauty's
the name of the *scientist*, actually. Gulping
horse at the head end means he pumps
out hay at the arse. 'Hay pressed-o!' he shrieks
to nervous applause. Oh for some bolts, oh

for a bow. But he's no Sagittarius, no. Half
Libra, half Gemini: a tough couple of births.
He rarely remembers which came first
in the Year of the Second Opinion.
It isn't immensely important. His lovers
feed him sugar lumps or are arrested. Twilight:
a coin-spinner guillotines tiny sandwiches.

Aubade

So sad. The sun stops giving the horizon head,
and rises... What a place to raise children. Or the dead.

Once risen they'll remark on time's grains of digital sand.
Querulously. But for now let such complaints be banned

– he said, imperiously. But seriously. For now take my fingers for torsos,
those of corpses trampled by steeple-chasing horses

and needing to be washed, cradled. For they're unable
to leave you thus uncoupled by the bedside table

beside the bed, unmade: they've read in your palm a mass
grave, its lifeline built on a fault line; a maze

in a killing field. How brave we are! How brave!
How saved! I pour my grave into your grave.

Any more equal and we'd be a minus.
Any sort of sequel would be an unwanted kindness.

Let us not seize the day by which we'll soon enough
be seized; let us forget how to breathe;

let us be motionless in our emotional urgency.
Let's not yet see, as if coming around mid-surgery,

the parting-poem blur between our eyes like a scalpel,
feel its downward drag like the tree in the apple,

or have it tip off the tips of our tongues like the nipple
towards which, fingers locked, we might appear to grapple

as we pray to the trickster Christ of the Infancy Gospel.
This clasp is the chapel. These digits the steeple-chasing people.

Animal Testing, Testing...

The satellites of love are at half power.
And charging. Oink. This isn't war, it's race
hate: listen, what we need is plenty space.
Like castoffs – blastoff! – of the water bear,

these satellites are in their element
where elements themselves would fare with dread.
If only slightly differently attired
we'd pass from distance for one planet mooned

to excess. Exes claim as much. Our axis
that tilts so far we make rotisserie
appear a pole dance... *c'est la vie*. It rocks us

to sleep as sound as great big rocks. Quite sound.
Our mutters are the sound of history
compelling piglets over mine-mined ground.

Art Forsaking Art

The graveyards back onto allotments here
and there. The cattle mourn the pastoral.
Their lowing is a kind of high: it thrills
the currents of the air. Young leaves it wor-

ries. Rising godlike with fists full of throat
as train wrecks plot their figures on a graph.
I don't identify with sociopaths.
It doesn't take a lot to get my goat.

The slavery museum in Liverpool:
a crude ceramic favouring abolition
is seeking thanks for having stayed its hand.

Its simple generosity seems failed.
Upon the sunshine, questions fall. Aspersions.
The sleet is also culturally determined.

Blues for Kaki King

If I could get these six strings working they still wouldn't work on you.
I'm entitled to exit at any point and everybody's glad when I do.

I have never listened to 'Wild Thing' and felt sorry for myself.
Thin cuts of wild thing fall off the freezer shelf.

Now we're going to do a cheer starting way way back at the back
of the room and moving to the front in an approximation of Barack

Obama's attack on all that his great nation holds dear. I hit
the road, Jack. I hit several deer. I listen to the hits. A bit

later I remember to steer. A piece of cake. A pissy piste.
Listen to my *scales*, Kaki: Louis MacNeice's little fish,

little *fishes*, circling the first hurdle, the second rate.
The happy finish: each left fin wings its way to the inevitable right,

the inalienable right bestowed upon those who ask more than once for
                                                            applause,
entitling everybody to exit through the big black backstage doors.

Blues for Marnie Stern

Before I woke this morning, I dreamed I rose by any other name.
Poetry's a preoccupation. I bought a new edition of the waiting game.

No dice. A shame. The single-sheet rulebook is missing a page.
Now I'm stuck exchanging puffs and puns with the watchful chronophage.

Its face is stocked with tics. To break it would be tygers burning Blake,
would be the book begging the self-publisher for *edits*, for heaven's sake,

would be the reciprocation of the love that seeketh wealth to please.
There's no time not to know your place. I smoke the breeze.

The chronophage smokes signals. Signet rings float on the river like,
·like, like cygnets.
Is that… is that right? *What value do yóu see in it?*

That's hard to say. The causeway's arm extends through mist, cattle, fox;
every drag rattles the bone-bag of the gear-shifts, the saddle, the padlocks.

'I' is what goes on without me. 'Marnie Stern': the stethoscope drilling
my chest.
It's not my heart rate but my listening speed that has of late increased.

Come

Come brioche, come briar, we make it to Cumbria.
Blood on the sheets. Something I'd rather leave
behind than find – meaning bloody sheets are like my bloody self.
I look down on my head's resemblance. Dartboard. Sombrero.

On cinnamon soil a farm cat gingers its blank belly.
The ghostly heft of famished heifers: *though your sins
be as scarlet*… Not heeding warnings today. I'm post-signs.
No newspapers is good. Holy is as holy does, pal…

What used to be right is now wed.
The sheep in their sheet-dresses, bullet-holed;
centuries of dark-muffled grasp-ache, here held.
The window is widowing. Her pane a migraine of white.

If snow be white, it's snowing. The flakes blush like shy men,
decline. Why then her breasts are done and dusted. Why then.

Dirge

for Jo

When you think about me, do you think: 'about seventeen'?
I'm as old as some hills. I'm alive with eyes. I'm the real thing,

a.k.a. the most convincing fake. The water it takes
to tranquillise me recalls, in its quantity, lakes.

Fish eat fish as flakes, while in my bigger tank I'm so
stuffed with my flaked skin my sinews are ceasing to show,

so sibilant with longing I'm background radiation,
that steady underglow. So ancient I forget the creation.

Notion will rise against notion, although we hate the idea; and
that ground opens up although holy is evident. But it's a lake's crater,
                                                            every dent:

one facet lit better can be most convincingly faked by all matter.
It's faith, or whatever. (The latter.) It's seed, or whatever, that which
                                                            we scatter.

Ashes make flashes on the sainted sand. We're singing
in the grains. We're ringing in the right sides of the wrong ones.

Down the Ringing Grooves

after Tennyson

I ain't saying she's a bonedigger. But by the moon in the doglight,
the fogbow… she robs your sea-grave. Why? God knows. (… Delete.

Behave. Be brave. Leave the gods to their every sparrow…) Spring!
When a young man's fancy lightly turns to something harrowing.

Spring, and the ways are narrowing: the crowds of wet, the currents of rot,
recede; flushed fen asserts itself against unflooding road,

and outlines ripen in the turned-up gleam's new focus.
That means: all life's on watch and guard. Inversion: my *operandi modus*.

Like a beast with lower back pains, though I say *the crescent*
promise of my spirit has not set, I cannot but resent

the ease with which the burial goods were dredged up
from the slush of the late year's descent, and the job

that I now have: pickaxing and C-4ing the scape's thick ridge
for the bygone against which she, seafarer, unknowingly brushed.

Life in Stolen Moments

I
Although atop the motte I am heir to the air-built castle,
　　they do call it a short swift slide from the mound of Venus to
　　　　　　　　　　　　　　　　　　　　　　　　the asshole.

II
I would dig like a dog to bury this bone-parcel
　　and grow something back to life from the germ of its own fossil.

III
Or set the skull to sea as its own vessel,
　　its self-portrait wrapped around the wind like a muzzle.

IV
This is a day if ever there was one to wrestle
　　with the dead things' commitment to the promised razzle-

V
dazzle of elsewhere. Here in the flavourless sizzle-
　　free land of the living one might puzzle

over the taste involved in the scratch and scrawl of trees' brown-dry bristles
    and wonder if the picture they press is worth the hassle,

VII
were it not for a sky so close being less a canvas than an easel
    against which this ellipsoid leans, pinned by pylons and seagulls.

Matthew

poetry's part of your self
      – Frank O'Hara

or a gift from God. God's gift to you might be that you are God's gift.
The message on mý T-shirt makes that T seem more a crucifix:

I SPILLED MY GUTS FOR YOU PEOPLE AND ALL YOU GAVE
                             ME WAS THIS.
See, not to show off but I grew up enjambing the two parts of the confess-

ional. My mind a grille. What goes in one ear comes out 'Mother,
I am stranded here on one side of what I think is a river,

and could never forgive myself for failing to be the leader
of men from the supercontinent to the isle of alders.' The grille is a ladder,

and although that grass might not be greener I am somebody who believes
us all entitled to believe ourselves laid upon its leaves.

I can tell you can tell I am very well informed. I write no sonnets;
do not attempt to second-guess me. For 'no sonnets' read 'one sonnet':

otherwise what hope in explaining the beautiful
woman's being beautiful like a bridge is beautiful?

Muse

That's an ankle bracelet, yes, but you don't háve an ankle.
Or so it appeared, paddling as you were in the inkwell.

A fetter of correcting fluid I spied, and misidentified. I'd let
you walk all over me – you'd leave huge   ing indents –

but for this need to live out the meaning of my creed.
By sleeping in my feed. You must have worked hard

not to have heard of Billie Holiday before your mid-thirties.
I border on impressed. A strange fruit hangs just south of my knees.

Which is very low. Daringly so. Hence out I go, out on my limbs,
two of them, initially... *What, in an interim, winces and limps?*

ponders the Sphinx. An errant ibis climaxes in its nostril.
The punchline's cudgel's an iron bar. Who would dare cross it? Al-

one in my bed, and well fed, I get to the other side. On days
ladies die I set alight a black flag. This is for cowardice.

Overhang

I can't kaleidoscope with the shame in my rainbones.
The hangover poem blocking, petty, out the stars:
a drum-tight close-up of *La cour du domaine du Gras*
graining the eyeball militarily. Megaphones.
By 'stars' one means the mute infinity of the sun's
being *yariganna*'d into winding-sheet-slender
escalopes that rim, corona, this vast game-ender
that backs the body against all that stammers, hums, errs.

Phantom

Walking as through tundra. Untrue land.
We hug against the smug wind and we speak
of fire, and fucking pigs. While holding hands.
I think it might be nice to be a pig.

Ta-daa. Of such things one is not to speak.
And one is not to wrench thus for the metre.
You count its toes like so: 'This little pig
is guilty only of *attempted* murder,

this merely of consuming its own meat;
this third one of misapprehending Orwell.
This fourth obeyed a plausible lack of order.
And this one weighed its home against a pearl

and cast home pitwards...'
                                Lash me to the wheel.
I need to know the swell, the strain. – *Oh hear
us when we cry to thee / for those in peril
on the sea* – A sea of freeze. A spear

between the ribs. Your heft of breath. I hear
the ring at the end of the note. I raise a hand
a touch too late, as if conducting pierced,
as if this treeless north were woodwind-lined.

The Bone Fire

Well-dressed good-time guys and dolls caught *in flagrante*,
hot under the collar in the land of plenty,

dusting the body of the bone fire for keepsakes,
keeping our insides warm with swigs from a hipflask.

You discarded a dog skull, its tongue black ribbon,
and dug deeper, settling on a horse's thighbone,

which you'd use for a year as splint, taper, poker,
a ward against death, a sword put through the Púca.

The good pickings were gone when at last I plucked up
my fledgling feathers and put it in my pocket:

a small claw that crooked too much like a man's finger
for comfort. It thrummed at my thigh, warm nail-ember,

and I trekked to the heart of a conifer wood
and scratched your name, birthing smokestumps and loud fireweed.

Caoilinn Hughes

I recently asked my students – who are predominantly Dutch, then German, Belgian, Polish, Turkish, Latvian, Luxembourgian and English – to bring in their favourite poem. Nearly half of the students arrived empty-handed. They had 'never read any poetry' and so they had no favourite. (This wasn't even opportunistic laziness!) 'But how are you okay with that? Tread softly now, folks, for you tread…' I made stabbing gestures at my heart. 'Are you not *aggrieved* for all that you've missed?' I have very little time for patriotism, but I did feel glad then to have come through the poems-arc-in-the-national-guts-whether-ye-like-it-or-not Irish school system. To me, poetry isn't just educational and sustaining and metaphysical and an aetheist's proxy to prayer; it's necessary. I haven't the slightest idea why, of course, but I've recently been obsessed with trying to work out poetry's value. *Perhaps it's a very small waste of everyone's time?* goes the refrain of the inner villain-elle. In writing, I try to work against that threat of irrelevance all the time (in my fiction too). I feel some foolish responsibility to the adult who has never read a poem, so that, just in case, just on the off-chance that they read one, it pulls its weight. I suppose what I'm saying is that I write for a reader. I believe poems need to be read, read aloud, experienced, and returned to again and again like addictive, mood-altering songs.

Estuary

Our arms are full of other people's babies: the shapeless
oyster fleshes of becoming. Nucleotides flood our laps, girdle
our wrists. Our mouths are full of cooing, cawing serenade.
'A pearl', we smile. We must take to this tender pink like tourists,
handling the toss of heads: *how privileged we are we are*
we are so prevailing in our choices. We go shoeless.
We collapse our sneezes into our chests. We do not let on
at the gutters of our bodies – we are hollow gastropod shells.

They observe our course, unfastened hands, whose only charms
are the scars of riverbeds, carnal somersaults, solitaire calluses.
Do we know what lies ahead? All lives come to an estuary,
in time. In their dancing eyes the world contracts to a coil:
a single dark loop quivering like all the bulged lips;
primed to suck, to kiss everybody in.

Catechism

Imagine sets of knees aching over the long Rosary,
praying for the conversion of Russia with glassy beads.

My aunt cried 'Up the Reds!' between Hail Marys
and was sent to bed. It might have been half-deliberate

when she snagged the sacrament, launching Glory Bes
into the gluey hives and trenches of her head,

never to be recovered. The floor cannot be knelt spotless.
The confetti falling from skies is shards of anklebone,

flickers of Phantom, the fragile metal feathers of an Albatros.
What is this moral, she might have pled, that draws us in –

like the bead to the stricture of its thread –
like the inevitable torso to the gleaming sword.

On Bringing the Common Cold to Tahiti

I

We are really only in transit.
This is not our honeymoon;
we don't believe in marriage, even if we do
believe in honeymoons but, what with moving costs,
our budget is anaemic and you can't have –
'The chicken or the egg?'
the air hostess asks, smiles, askance.
I wonder if I should tell her about the palpitations.
I request another envelope of those satirical crackers
and one more pinot chopine to add to my bag.
I've been stockpiling them because we have no French
Polynesian Francs and someone needs to lend the recession culture.

'Welcome to the Isle of *Tahiti*' plays on rerun
as we land, stressing unseemly syllables like party lines.
At the dock, we turn down taxis. We drag Stuff
behind us, along with fishhook thumbs.
Our language contains most of the things
we want to keep of our lives. Our luggage
contains the effects no one bid on on Trademe
or were undivvy-outable: spare scratched reading glasses;
branded bath towels and mugs from my corporate time;
wall hangings that double as rugs; the plastic-
stringed chirango that even Johnson couldn't make sing.
It's all grievously dowithoutable.

I ask our third lift – a Breton – in fauché fran-
çais what brings one to migrate to such an island.
He came avec vacance as a thirty-something and brought home
an adopted son who, once grown, gathered his belonging from Europe.
Regard this *grave* economic disparity, he states. 'It is something
my son could not reconcile. Look what we have!'
(I think my favourite wine is *Grave*.) I see, I say. It's more Samoa
                                                                than France.
'Before or after the tidal wave?'
We are not on honeymoon. We have been packing

our lives up, binding theses, PDFing CVs, zip-
filing our relationships. Do you have astigmatism? I enquire.
I have all sorts of lenses. Do you still see your son?

II

No one can take us to where we are staying,
because we only have a vague idea. But we have come
to terms with this. Moor'ea is completely beautiful.
Mountains, beaches, coral reefs, cups with brown-breasted
women going on the cheap. There are no chested bare
women going on the cheap that I know of.
It's hard enough being female, taking flight. We are alone
in our hostel as it is cheap and on a backwater
mud bank. White sandless. Still, you only need to swim
a while to trace elements of paradise. But we fall sick
as dogs and everything tastes of smashed porcelain
because I ground my crown to crackleware in my sleep;
even the poison cru Chinois we buy from a roadside cart
after walking a mile in the dog-ridden gloom has flavours of china.

Our host is maybe confounded by us. He's hard to read.
We are not on honeymoon. We are sick.
Will you hire surfboards? We are *very* sick. What will you do?
Well, I checked my email and I have an interview
(I say I'm a teacher, as my sinuses are unwriterly, and being
an academic is academic – the fever is advancing! – no, it's just, the truth
is awkwarder) so I must write a Statement of Teaching Philosophy.
Will you take the outrigger canoe that I built?
Or the bikes? (We blow our noses.) What will you do?
My not-fiancé says that he will read *Voltaire's Bastards*.
What is it? It's really a disillusionment with the Age of Reason
in general, he says. This is why I'm ashamed.
I give my not-fiancé a dirty look. He adds: I'll also read *The Martian*.
It's like MacGyver, but in Space! But you are in Tahiti?

'My wife and child went to the dock. They got on a boat and they left.'
I translate this to French and back again in my head,
but it is no less alarming. I slap a mosquito from my neck

and feel wet–cloth–headed. My breathing sounds of vinyl.
I offer Tama a pinot chopine and *Air Tahiti Nui* Craisins.
He seems hard done by by our staring at Windows
rather than out of windows, but these colds
weren't brought on by any kind of draught; we have endless duties.
Besides, it is urgent that we find somewhere to live online.
'Which flag for you? I put up flags for guests' countries.'
Are we talking loyalties? There's the two of us, so we settle on five.
'Have you Stated your Philosophy?' he asks. Nearly. I have the *phileo*,
meaning *to love* or *to befriend*. 'Oh. You want postcards to send?'
No, no, there's the two of us. We can just... We wave our tissues.

The ocean hunkers like a self-possessed athlete,
as Tama drives us to the ferry; it's like *The Picture of Dorian Gray* –
a closed blue-jacketed hardback – all coral, incorrigible beauty beneath.
Tama is silent. The radio plays 'Welcome to the Isle of *Tahiti*'
quietly and we pretend it sounds different now
that we are leaving, meaning closer to arriving; now
that we have passed to the less feverish side of a Doppler shift.
In Dutch, I propose to my unfiancé: would it be *vreemd, onbeleefd*
to gift Tama a used Google beach towel? The conditional tense
takes him aback. We are getting somewhere! We have all sorts of things
to say, to teach, if we are called upon. 'What is this sickness?'
Tama rasps, finally. 'What do you do to make it go away?' He has paled.
We were nearly there, nearly gone. The flags had been dismantled.
I look around, for a woman, *Sophia*, or an orphan on the dock.

We Are Experiencing Delay

We are experiencing a delay due to a body on the tracks
the broadcaster drones. Fluid pools in lower limbs that have been disowned.
A body is experiencing delay among the ballast and the black.

We throttle our tabloids like pillowcases, as if to rid the newscasts
of their creases, though headlines cannot compete with the coroner megaphone.
We are experiencing delay due to a body on the tracks.

No one is reading a love letter behind a Henry James hardback.
Neither sympathies, books nor lovers have been taken out on loan.
A body is experiencing delay among the ballast and the black.

Aside sleepers, we search Perseus's shield for cracks:
we see our sorry forms in darkened perspex. We are not as we are shown.
We are experiencing delay due to a body on the tracks.

Home is an idea that comes and goes. The idea is carried on our backs;
now silk-lined, now boned. All there is of its embodiment are steppingstones.
A body is experiencing delay among the ballast and the black.

There will be no tombstone in the landscape for a page marker, for a fact.
The speaker intones: We will not be long. Headlines, epitaphs: He is not alone.
We are experiencing a delay due to a body on the tracks.
A body is experiencing delay among the ballast and the black.

Apple Falls from the Tree

after Gregor Johann Mendel (1822–1884)

I

Place in two untiring hands as many hectares of monastery garden;
breed, mongrelise, tally, catalogue with obedience, self-discipline,
three dozen pea species; cultivate the principles of heredity.

Take the Liturgy of the Hours literally. Blot out all noise of Darwin,
for Goodnesse sake. Feed in silence at grave refectory tables; forgo tonguing
pea jackets from your teeth. Later, if you must, you may mutter

over careful protein register: round or wrinkled ripe seed shape;
green or yellow endosperm; white or purple petal colour; pods pinched
or ballooned; dwarfed or drawn-out stem; flower position axial or terminal.

Kneel in your tunic, cincture; stoop in hooded shoulder. Produce the effect
of labouring for the Kingdom of Heaven. Pray unceasingly for
the world, *quidem*.
Unsoil the spirit. Rest when you fall down. Only then, take earth scent
in, in moderation.

Free education should not be taken lightly. Especially when Physics has
been chosen
over Hermeneutics. Nay! Your class of observation need not entail the
fornication of mice!
Plants should display equally the discontinuity of atom, God's good
benefaction.

II

And yet your work is incomplete and unconvincing. What's this, about
the presence
of absences? The *potential* is there in the germ, the gene, you say, and evident
in only one of three grandchildren. The Good Lord Jesus was *not* a blend
of his chaste parents?

Be that as it may, your research must be self-reflective – recessive.
Perhaps it will resurface
in some generations, after you have assumed the role of Abbott. Indeed,
yes, paperwork,
as much as robes, could snag, but you have amply proven hardihood.

III

Genius, as it were, must be – like God – invisibly existent. Just unexpressed,
for now, until He recrudesces. Perhaps your lifework will revivify from
the luckless bonfire,
unscathed; your papers, after all, did lie on Darwin's bookshelf when he
died; alas, uncut.

Transverse Orientation

To watch moths as a pastime is known as mothing.
Nothing is known about what makes one inclined to mother
or less inclined to that sort of glow
curio. Moth-er with
– unexpectedly –
the short O of body
rather than the O Oh of that longer load
zooming in on the veining
on the cleaving husk
the processionary male
you knew you know
before their moth-hood is realised
some of the worm-states don't even face
the slog of cocooning just dig
into the ground and stay there until it's all over.
Cooing toddlering plod. The codling
moth is only one named species among
tens of thousands that might have been mothered,
among the what-might-as-well-be-billions yet to be described.
Corn borers. Bullworms. The invasive gypsy moth.
Those sorts are boxed as bothers but it's a misnomer
that all moths pest. Many have no mouths
and do not eat at all never mind clothes. Those that do
favour white finely chopped mulberry leaves.
No one scorns the silk-makers though
as long as they issue forth good thread
from the tiny holes in their jaws.
A trait worth buoying. It seems
a pseudoscience that such finery could yield
from their drab powder forms. It would be a crime
not to foster it. Better to spew a fother of silken filaments
which can be carted off and bathed in troughs of luke
warm water (serving to soften the gum binding
so that the wombs can be unravelled and streamlined
to a skein of raw product) better that
than to spew out their own attributes or the quirks
of their run-of-the-mill species.

Why all this mothing, the spinning
round and round? There is a theory
it has something to do with the moon
that by keeping a regular angular relationship
with a luminous celestial body
moths can fly straight as bootlaces. The light
will always be above the skyline – looming.
Planets are so obvious, a loss of bearing would easily be corrected
they speculate.
But here. How to forge away – skirt an orbit?
She circles this screen   this page   this energy-saving bulb
closer and closer
spiralling in on the ultrasonic incidence
! plummets now !
a reflex as all this falls past her horizon.
Is it over?
Is this the moon?
Mothers usually sleep this time of day.

Communion Afternoon

I would have outsmarted them or, at a minimum,
flicked their coins back like sharp-edged playing
cards or swung the rosary beads like a Filipino Balisong
had I not vomited spaghetti alphabet all over the spring-time
grass and fake-white silk and girlhood; disgusted
at the injustice of being small and atheist and inarticulate.

God Always Geometrises

I measured the skies, now the shadows I measure.
Skybound was the mind, earthbound the body rests.
— *Johannes Kepler*

He was the first to stare at stars and really dream
of travelling. He gauged the radii between earths
and suns by careful estimation, deduction, thirst
of acumen. Mars was not a Hallowed warning but an Axiom.

He would navigate the Holy Spirit — space — between
God, seated upon Sol, and his Son: the astral musician.
He would bring back to earth a law of motion.
Veritas from Saturn. One must not become a libertine,

his mother warned, when he raved of the sublime
altitudes and began examining metaphysics
through a telescope at eleven, deciphering in the universe
designs far too arithmetical to be divine.

His father fled to the Netherlands, the Eighty Years' War,
never to return; so Katharina Guldenmann nursed
the parts of her son that could carry on fatherless, cursed.
Her shoulders were pilasters of thought. They would endure.

She held young Kepler's wafer frame up to the Great Comet;
to see the lunar eclipse that made the moon appear
reddened. He maddened at its indistinct picture.
His eyes were unreliable. Smallpox had rotted their promise.

It would take his own son by the throat and throttle
the life out of him like the conflict out of a paradox
one day. Then there would follow the soulless equinox.
But before those burdens that awaited him — the chattel

of creed; the death to spotted fever of a twice-widowed wife;
wasted labour; the trial of witchcraft he would bring upon his mother —
before all that strife, he dreamt of interstellar travel; the sonorous ether;
of hearing the harmony of the spheres, at the threshold of afterlife.

Harmony of the Spheres

for Johannes Kepler

Heaven knows the planets are not silent in their orbits.
They sound of swallows making cyclical migrations;
returning blue-feathered, quavering melancholic airs.

Though, Angelic unison is compromised on Earth
for we are not its audience: its song is directed Sunward.
A degree of alteration is required for melodic heirs.

Celestial orbs were placed by the Creator to balance
consonance with dissonance; discord with concord:
with each revolution resounds chromatic fanfares.

For the same reason, the seasons turn their backs:
the planets loom and whirl and leave the Sun, Moon, Earth
and we should heed the progression of Apostolic prayers.

The nature of all things observes the geometric compliment.
Even our eyes show the numeric inverse of His
cosmos in their rendering; a Soul therein the optic stares.

Equally, distance, velocity, hastening can be measured
in the triad of our wisdom. Father, Ephemeral Son, swan feather,
telescope: the semitones between us are rhapsodic lairs.

Life on Earth is fleeting, exhausting. Our griefs are swallows
lifting small wing chords. Thus, as passage migrants,
we too play our part in the great symphonic overture.

Nic Aubury

In his wonderful little *Introduction to English Poetry*, James Fenton quotes, and comments sagely upon, the assertion in the *Oxford Companion to English Literature* that 'Verse in the twentieth century has largely escaped the straitjacket of traditional metrics'. Perhaps it's because my understanding of what poetry is has its roots in the literature of Ancient Greece and Rome that I, like Fenton, am slightly mystified by the idea that metre might serve to constrain the poet; that we poets would somehow be able to say all the things we wanted to say if only our heads weren't in such a muddle with all those dratted iambs, trochees, amphibrachs and so on. From Homer and Virgil onwards, so much great poetry, written according to strict metrical patterns, makes a nonsense of this notion. In short, I think it's okay for poems to scan. Even more unfashionably, I also happen to think it's okay for poems – proper poems, I mean – to rhyme. I think it's okay for poems to be funny and accessible, too – populist, even. I don't think they always have to be, by any means, but I think it's okay when they are. This is certainly what my poems tend to be like, including the dozen or so in this anthology. I think that in a simple observation or even a silly little joke there can sometimes be quite a profound truth.

Bertrand Russell's Chicken

The man who has fed the chicken every day throughout its life at last wrings its neck instead, showing that more refined views as to the uniformity of nature would have been useful to the chicken.

— Bertrand Russell, *The Problems of Philosophy*

Each morning, he would cross the little yard
Which lay between the farmhouse and our shed,
And every day, the same slow, heavy tread
Of thick-soled work boots scuffing on the hard,
Brick path would let us know we'd soon be fed.
Then, chirping a falsetto 'Chook, chook, chook!'
He'd open wide the makeshift henhouse door,
Which scarred concentric arcs across the floor,
And scatter corn. It fell in every nook
And cranny; nestled down amongst the straw.
So how could we have known what he would do –
So quickly, too, before we'd understood
Quite what was happening? No – no one could.
The man that day was not the one we knew –
A simple husbandman whose heart was good.
He hasn't ever been that way again,
And things are back exactly as they were –
Except, of course, we all remember her.
And every day we hear his boots, and then
The door, the scattered corn, the others stir.

The mother of five reckons four was a breeze
Whilst the mother of four dreams of what she could do
As a mother of three (who would manage with ease,
So she says, if she'd stayed as a mother of two).
And the mother of two thinks the mother of one
Has the easiest time while bemoaning her lot,
For the number of children you need to have fun
Is exactly one less than the number you've got.

Decline and Fall

*(A cautionary tale which may or may not be sung to the tune
of Gilbert & Sullivan's 'Major General's Song')*

Homer wrote the *Iliad* and latterly the *Odyssey*
(One heroey-and-battley, one monstery-and-goddessy);
He's European literature's indubitable fountainhead
(Though, modestly, he'd claim it was those Muses on that Mount instead).
Then Homer was the model for the epic of Vergilius
(or 'Virgil' as we call him now, to sound less supercilious);
For centuries the world revered his masterful hexameters
But nowadays they fall outside curricular parameters.
For modern pedagogues, equating relevance with recency,
Eschew our ancient texts without propriety or decency
Resulting in a cultural and moral disinheritance
Which means that we're no better than the – OMG! – Americans.

Neither Barrel

A tut is the click that an Englishman makes
When, affronted, he's quick to react
And he fires a rebuke, but discovers too late
That his mouth wasn't loaded, in fact.

Rhyme Nor Reason

You can't rhyme 'plough' with 'cough' or 'rough',
Or 'thorough', 'through' or 'though';
Hough foreigners can learn this stough
I troughly wouldn't knough.

April Fool

He woke on the morning of April the first
And saw her, just standing there, already dressed
In her coat, with a bag and a speech she'd rehearsed:
'I'm leaving,' she said. 'I'll come back for the rest.'
Now, seven years on, he won't call her a bitch
Or resent her. He smiles; he's a reasonable bloke,
And he has to admire all the trouble to which
She has gone for the sake of a practical joke.

Moving

Before we lock the door and hit the road
I'm drawn inside again, and through the hall
My footsteps echo sharply. I survey
The ghosts of pictures stained on every wall
And carpets bleached with plans of rooms now stowed
In boxes and transported far away.

From room to empty room I strain to hear
A tiny sound from somewhere in the past
– A call to tea, some footsteps on the stair,
a cracker pulled, a radio, a blast
Of argument, a garden-football cheer –
But what was once is now no longer there.

Reflections on Piaf

What, *honestly*, Edith? *Rien de rien?*
No hint of remorse, or the slightest chagrin?
I'm pleased for you, truly, but faintly surprised:
My regrets are in volumes, and alphabetised.

Summer Calling

When teachers cite 'vocation' as the reason why they chose
A life imparting knowledge to our youth,
They are, as any educator past or present knows,
A vowel away from telling you the truth.

The Hunter-Gatherer

I zigzag slowly through the aisles
Of packets, tins and ready meals,
Past staff with here-to-help-you smiles
And signs proclaiming discount deals,
And while I'm weighing up my choice
Between some different tinned sardines,
From deep within, an ancient voice
Cries out: 'This can't be what it means
To be a man!' I turn, and then
A sudden notion fills my mind
To join my fellow shopping men,
To run outside, to leave behind
These bright, refrigerated shelves,
Where all our needs and wants are piled,
And hunt for vols-au-vent ourselves
And gather loo rolls in the wild.

A Good Innings

When he wearily climbed the pavilion stair,
He imagined he'd do so to sunlit applause.
There was drizzle and chill in the late-season air
When he wearily climbed the pavilion stair;
Just a handful still watched (although none seemed to care
About all of his singles and sixes and fours).
When he wearily climbed the pavilion stair,
He'd imagined he'd do so to sunlit applause.

Start As You Mean To Go On

I cannot hide the joy I feel
In undertaking something new;
My starts are always full of zeal,
A cheerful will to see things through.

In undertaking something new
I rarely plan, just dive straight in;
A cheerful will to see things through
Takes hold of me as I begin.

I rarely plan, just dive straight in.
Then boredom, mixed with mounting dread,
Takes hold of me as I begin
To understand what lies ahead.

Then boredom, mixed with mounting dread
And waning vigour, presses me
To understand what lies ahead:
An end of assiduity.

And waning vigour presses me;
The wind is taken from my sails.
An end of assiduity;
My last enthusiasm fails.

The wind is taken from my sails
And, throwing in the towel, it's true
My last enthusiasm fails.
I need to look for something new.

And, throwing in the towel, it's true,
I cannot hide the joy I feel.
I need to look for something new;
My starts are always full of zeal.

J. Kates

Biographical and compositional details go into writing, but these are like the booster stage of an interplanetary rocket, to be dropped behind (harmlessly, we hope) once the real thing is launched to its destination. And a writer's own commentary is like the contrail: no matter how pretty it looks, it pollutes the atmosphere.

Orientation

I know a scoter from a coot,
a common eider from a king.
I know what song the mute swan sings
(I'll bet you know it isn't mute).
I know a harrier on the wing
and followed one one afternoon

in mid-October through the mud
and bitter milkweed of the moor
until I lost it in the air
and lost myself on lower ground
while rainclouds gathered overhead
around an early rising moon.

I knew I wasn't far from home.
I knew I wasn't really lost.
Less than a mile from the coast
(I didn't know it at the time)
the county road is paved and posted
and when the wind is blowing west

the rain will hold off for a while.
Somewhere to the east you waited –
you didn't know I would be late.
I climbed up on a little hill
to try to get my bearings straight,
then started off the way I guessed.

I would have liked you at my side.
You know how to interpret clues
and find the things I always lose
or unintentionally hide.
You know the lore I could have used
if looking did me any good.

Three kinds of heather, two of pine,
a dogfish and a basking shark,
a fritillary and a monarch
catch all the light the sun can shine
but fade to darkness in the dark.
I stumbled home. I knew I could.

Schein: A Toast

*[Shine] combines the ability of the physical hero with the verbal skill of the trickster
or pimp hero. Shine cracks jokes as he swims away from the sinking ship and drowning
whites; he ends up safely on dry land in orgies of sex and booze. [...] He finishes best
of all, for he has not only women but everything money can buy.*
                                    – Bruce Jackson, *"Get Your Ass in the Water and Swim
                                            Like Me": Narrative Poetry from Black Oral Tradition*

1

Schein played the fiddle and Schein could dance
to any old tune with elegance.

What would pious folk believe
if they saw the girls Schein met in Kiev?

Schein made money and Schein made love
to every skirt in Chernigov.

Schein trimmed the corners of his beard
and climbed on a train while the shtetl cheered.

Schein traded off with a cossack chieftain
a new gold watch for his old black caftan.

Schein's tefillin went into hock
for a silver-handled alpenstock.

2

Schein was out on the street one day
when a shaygetz tried to block his way

who wore the badge of the tsar's Black Hundreds,
spat like a Turk and stared and thundered.

Said Schein, 'You look like a schmuck too dumb
to find your way to your own pogrom.'

When the goy decided to take a piss,
Schein treated him to an instant bris.

3

Schein got as far as Petrograd
where he met the Tsar for smorgasbord.

Schein took Rasputin out for dinner
and ate pork chops with the holy sinner.

After Schein's Imperial schmooze,
Reb Romanoff cried, 'God save the Jews!'

Schein got involved in politics
till Lenin came by with the Bolsheviks.

Schein hid Anastasia in a mikvah –
Now in Haifa she sings *Hatikvah*.

Babel shut up and Bronstein fled,
Mandelstam starved and Mikhoels bled,

But Schein was shtupping a commissar's wife
and couldn't be bothered to lose his life.

4

Schein was in Dresden on Kristallnacht
and yelled with the rest, 'Deutschland Erwacht!'

Schein took a trip to Berchtesgarten
and climbed to the castle belching and farting.

Schein in a Stube talked mamaloshen
and paid for his beer with counterfeit groschen.

Schein made a deal with Oskar Schindler –
– one was a gonif, the other a swindler –

They bought up lampshades, soap and glue
and made them into an Ersatz Jew

Schein sold to the Krauts for ready cash, then
spent it all on hamentashen.

5

Schein fitted a ship for Palestine
and filled it full of kinderlein.

When the British boarded in fear and panic,
Schein said, 'This is better than the *Titanic*',

jumped in the water and swam for shore
like his doppelgänger had done before.

Schein landed in Eretz Yisroel
said, 'Nuts to this', and took to his heels.

He came to the Statue of Liberty,
said 'Hey, Big Mamma, you're for me.'

Next you know, there were girls with torches
and kids with schnozzolas on Iowa porches.

6

Schein says only trees have roots.
Yids have legs and leather boots.

The Ax-Murderer's Daughter

The ax-murderer's daughter
got a brand-new yellow tutu
and satin slippers
for her eighth birthday.

And today is Every-Other-Saturday:
time to visit with her mother
where he lives ever since the accident
she was too young to remember
almost.

How she hates the long drive,
the iron doors and corridors,
the dirty little room where three bored men
watch her mother talking to him,
two girls fidgeting.

What is she supposed to think
about the stranger she's supposed to love
for her mother's sake and Jesus'?

She will stop visiting when she goes away to college
but write faithfully every month.

He will learn about her own two children, her divorce,
her move out of state, her new home.

She will give instructions to the chief of police
(there is always talk of budget-cutting,
of letting the safe ones out)
if ever he shows up in town:
Shoot on sight.

But today she will dance for him
in the dirty metal room to canned music
borrowed from her teacher.
She will wear her yellow tutu and satin slippers,
her mother, sister watching
and three bored guards.

And he will watch her, too, saying afterwards,
my little girl.
      That's my little girl.

Learning to Shoot

My father leaned on a fence post
a hard stone's throw from empty cans
balancing on a rock wall
or hung like Christmas ornaments
against the backdrop of a hill.

I pressed the stock into my cheek,
settled the tiny knob bobbing
on the barrel's lip to its wide V.
My left wrist ached with the burden
of holding steady, my right index

finger practiced the art of being
gentle and precise. Pocked cans
spun, swayed, leaped backward
out of sight. The dead hill echoed.
One big one bled a little green paint.

Winter, deer came down to the garden,
beveled the apple twigs, stripped rhododendron.
In summer, I dreamed of camping out
in the meadow above the poison ivy
to watch them run by moonlight.

★

Suddenly they stop downwind, alert,
poised in their dappled hideouts –
mark me as one to shy off from
as if they catch the glint of a thought
and know better than I, my aim.

Out

Everything will, you know. The bone
harp singing in the king's hall,
the cunning wound, tobacco-stained
carpeting, a telephone call,

Col. Mustard in the dining-room
with a wrench, Raskolnikov
in existential gloom,
brothers wrestling over a pocketknife

on a slippery riverbank,
strangers stretched on their knees.
Fingering a pistol, jilted Frankie
nails Johnnie in his BVDs.

That's how it is: What we act
in private becomes the matter
of music, the marrow of related fact
in a storyteller's patter,

and nothing we can dream is left
without beforehand or afterwards
unaccounted for. When we laughed,
our laughter was broadcast by the birds,

and when you slammed the door
an old shaman in a weatherbeaten tent
half the world away finished the story
and told me where you went.

The Uses of Poetry

for Larry Joseph

Don't tell me poetry makes nothing happen.
I had your verse in front of me, was reading,
to be precise, about a black boy bleeding
in Detroit, the poem 'I Think About Thigpen
Again', my country window thrown wide open
to the October wind because I needed
air and daylight, when like a double-beaded
black bullet a single hornet flew right in.
Out here, people pack their handguns, too,
but, given the odds, I'm far more apt to die
by being stung than being shot. What do I do,
who love all innocent creatures? The hornet shook
its iridescent wings and settled down. I
whopped it dead with your compassionate book.

At Starfire Lake

In love with someone else,
I lay back not alone —
a blanket on a stone
underneath our elbows —

and looked without regret
at the end of day.
Whatever was to say
was already said.

Where the shoreline curved,
a single heron flew
slowly out of view.
She and I observed

a pointlessly opaque
twilight in the sky
over the idle eye
of a flat, gray lake.

The First Muse

Adam had wandered off. Loneliness hissed
insinuating in her ear a line
so insistent she could not resist,
repetitive, recoiling, serpentine.

She mouthed a name. She hummed a note. She cut
a caper, kicking up red dirt. She saw
stars overhead. She wept. She laughed. She thought.
If there was *now*, then there had been *before*.

Adam came back. She tried to clue him in.
He heard her out. He doubted her at first
and came up with a new locution, *sin*.
But she refuted. Let God do His worst,

with every breath she had the best of it.
The man inhaled. Inspired, he plucked and bit.

Winterlied

The low sun lights from underneath
a coming snow sky.
A crow alone cries to a crow alone
in a nearby tree –
a few flakes thicken the air.

Here's to those who sit by their own fire,
and here's another to warm the feet
of those who set out tonight
and get from here to there
before the morning.

And here's the last of what we have
for those of us with nowhere to go
who come as well from nowhere –
you on the wing, already shaking snow,
I in a nearby tree.

Words

after V.S. Rabenchuk

I write. I command. The word is an animal
to the truth — sometimes a flower or stone
or star, you say? — no, always a beast, and one
it's up to each of us to bring to heel.

I track words through their laughter and their tears.
I crack my whip and order them: Be divine!
Love one another! They snarl and pace the line
and ravage a carrion meal when it appears.

I watch them fly in chevrons overhead
looking for quiet waters. I set out
decoys to bring them close enough to shoot.
After the first, even the last has fled.

I lie in wait among the quiet reeds
for a word to swallow the hook, come flashing up
like sunrise and flap gasping in the scupper.
Dying, the scales turn gray; a small mouth bleeds.

Rebecca Watts

I wrote these poems between 2010 and 2013. Some are driven simply by observations and images I wanted to communicate; others are the necessary consequences of external events (namely, bats flying into my bedroom). While I hope they can all be read without introduction, here are a few acknowledgements: 'Observations on Marriage' paraphrases a section of David Attenborough's commentary from episode two of *The Blue Planet* (BBC, 2005); a 'German Tinder Box, c.1800' used to sit on the mantelpiece in William Wordsworth's former home, Dove Cottage, where I worked for a while as a tour guide; and 'Letter from China' was inspired by a passage in Steven Pinker's book *The Better Angels of Our Nature* (Allen Lane, 2011).

The Molecatcher's Warning

Nobody asked or answered questions out there.
Ten miles from the nearest anywhere
the landscape was a disbanded library.

Only the moles remained
strung on a barbed wire fence,
a dozen antiquated books forced open.

It must've been the north-east wind
or a bandit crow starved of familiar company
that picked them over so –

not a scrap hanging on
inside the stretched, taupe skins,
their spines disintegrating.

Read in me
they wanted to declare
how it all ends.

But the threads which once
had a hold on their soft hearts
dangled, loose and crisp.

And their kin
can't read anything
but earth.

Turning

Now it's autumn
and another year in which I could leave you
is a slowly sinking ship.

The air has developed edges
and I am preparing to let myself lie
in a curtained apartment,

safe in the knowledge that strangers
have ceased to gather and laugh
in the lane below

and the brazen meadow no longer
presumes to press its face to the window
like an inquisitor.

Soon even the river will evince a thicker skin,
my breath each morning will flower white,
and all of summer's schemes will fly like cuckoos.

The leaves are turning and the trees
are shaking them off. Bonfire smoke
between us like a promise lingers.

Letter from China

Bare branches prick the landscape.

It is not the force of nature
that holds the country in perpetual winter

but the facts of arithmetic
and a fear of winter.

Ask the elderly,
they know what life costs:

once forced to sow seeds,
eyes fixed on the future,

they envisaged themselves
slipping into the river of old age

and reckoned
that a son could keep them afloat

but a daughter is like
spilled water.

So it was
that those who reached the light were dealt with

quickly, shushed
in a bucket beside the bed,

while those whom fortune allowed to be glimpsed
curled in the dark womb

were dislodged, dug out, disposed of
before they could begin to flower;

to make way for boys with stronger shoulders,
fit to carry parents.

This was the calculation.
That was their hope.

Now we live in a lopsided sum,
looking onto a wilderness

where scores of unsettled men
conspire:

bare branches
on which our future hangs.

Hopeless together, they clamour for fire.

Visitor

I find myself standing in the garden
among familiars: pink and yellow roses;
an anniversary bird-bath now wrapped in moss;
the stone-grey football that gathers water
and wheezes like an old man. On the ridged path
loose soil shifts between my toes.

I reach over the back fence, unbolt the gate,
sidestep the fat blackcurrant bush
and weave through avenues of runner beans.
In the heat of the greenhouse, time breathes
slowly, the air heavy as tomatoes;
the same air that hung about your hands.

I make an inventory: cracked flowerpots;
radio components awaiting reincarnation;
spilt seeds still clinging to dreams of geraniums.
I close the door. The sun stays inside, dozing.
In the shade of the laburnum your collection of rain
is brimming again. I deliver it. It keeps returning.

Insomniac

Midnight.
Sky hung like ink in a jar of water.
Moon smooth as a glacier mint on its way to dissolution.

Walking the towpath
cheeks pale
I am dissolving

but not in the way I seek;
not as the mind's fingers reach out
and fuse with the fingers of sleep

to cradle eight hours of dreams; more
as the line between solid and liquid
might be rubbed out,

as path tree grass bench bin everything
blurs. Amid the vagaries
of unsleep

the spirit of the old city is rising like damp,
feeling its blind way back to the fens,
groping at my face and lungs. Here

river has taken to air,
let go of silt,
shrugged off houseboats and swans

to hover over its essence:
to kiss me. When
all I want

is everything to slot into
its proper place:
flat sky, round moon, straight path, dark river.

To lie down still as a woman between new sheets:
eyes closing effortlessly, mind empty
as a jar of water.

German Tinder Box, c.1800

Here's day awaiting itself without realising,
holed up on the mantelpiece in a souvenir tin.
It smells of old conspiring coins:
the morning's tender. Inside it's restless,
flinching in snug dark, dreaming of fire.

Waking is never easy: it happens gradually
with metal, oil, rag, splint; from the patient
clock, clock, clock of flint on flint
a spark is drawn and flown on a paraffin flag
till dawn's incensed, and left to burn.

A box worth more than its weight in gold,
once they learned the European magic:
to see their own sun born and lifted
out of the heart of a black forest.

Lodge Farm

Sixteen years will have shifted since the night we stood
with the moon and an unhitched wagon of pumpkins in the yard,
coat sleeves pushed up over our elbows, breath like spirits.
Our big knives twisted and sliced, cleaved flesh to make bone,
hollowed eyes. We scooped mulch out in palmfuls and set aglow
a line of gormless faces, each one insensible of its loss.

Now it's September and we're stooped in rows in the orchard,
the last of the low sun on our shoulders, cheeks russetted,
tossing windfalls into buckets. Later we'll take turns at the table:
halve, crush and shovel the fruit into your grandfather's wooden box,
press down the lid, borrow a man to turn the crank; watch as the liquid
pools in the gulley, spills over and is funnelled into fat glass bottles.

We'll collect a cupboard-full and wait; look forward; light a bonfire, stand about and talk until we're stood in the dark and suddenly wonder when the sun went down. Then some philosopher ablaze on last year's cider will look up and say *that's how it goes* – we remember the sun and the dark, not the day growing old. It's overlooked, what happens in the middle. Like the browning of an apple once it's bitten.

Observations on Marriage

Lucky he – little angler fish
who finds another in vast emptiness
ambivalence impossible
they fuse – symbiotic
so never let go

On land, though
before that bold witness, the sun
how does she lure him?
what chemicals ride the air between
to hook him on a scented thing?
a self no better than himself
(her blood circulating in her body)
(his blood circulating in his body)
two bodies long distanced from the void
lifted far above deep sea – yet
craving parity – compelled
to attach permanently

proposals breach skin
like a bite on the belly

marine snow makes
beautiful
confetti

Two Bats

The first I met was a baby,
an accidental landing on the pillow.
Four floors up, the night was hot
and the window wide and receptive as an eye.
Though it hadn't meant to come, its two short flights
cast suspicion on the room, before it joined us, trembling.
In the lamplight it was little more than fur and wing,
no bigger than a thumb; a pulse. Humbled,
it held still as we slid the pint-glass under
then raised it slowly to the moon.

The second was sent. Full-grown,
it knew its way around the landscape better than I
who'd thrown the sash down early to inhale the view
and been carried away across moors –
so the creature slipped in at dusk unnoticed.
When I hit the switch for the big light
it flung itself back and forth above our heads,
a glove, issuing a challenge over and over.
No instincts rose. Perhaps we were too familiar;
perhaps we already knew that if it settled
we'd be repulsed by black eyes, thin wings,
bared teeth like a little man's. Instead,
we waited sheepishly on the landing
not looking at much, while someone else
nobler with a tea-towel dealt with it.
Afterwards, though we were left to sleep,
something hung on in the dark between us.

Emmeline's Ascent

Back when her kind should've kept
the fact of ankles to themselves,
it was mildly surprising:
that from the ground – where her

neat boots were tied with satin bows
and her knees, unremarked-on, stood
fixed beneath a triple skirt and had not
one single scar to boast of – she

thought to ascend the small stepladder
borrowed for the job from someone's father
and, loosely grasping the hand of a stranger,
swing brilliantly from the hip one long

athletic leg over the rim, into unsupported
territory, without even a pale second
given over to the fear of falling the five
shameful feet back to zero, from such

a high wheel; and that once in the saddle
she recognised herself seeing not what
she never before could've imagined,
but everything exactly as it was – the

clear hard road, made for going along;
the terraces lined up for her admiration;
and on the other side of the clipped hedge
the unhatted men in the park, a few streets

but fantasies away from closed offices,
airing the first hint of their balding crowns
to the pigeons and anyone else geared up
for once to peer down on them from above.

Obsession

As your voice pulls away down the line
I picture you. It's warm, and the baby
is in bed, indifferent to daylight,
dreaming of you even while you
confound her imagination.

You are not clearing away the lunch things
or ironing cricket whites for Saturday.
On the carpet the animal alphabet waits
for the sequel to Jellyfish, while other colourful
objects lie mute in the dark under the sofa.

You're standing at the window, transfixed,
as *Columba livia*, estranged from the rocks,
alight in your grid of cabbages.
The motley rabble's nodding insatiably,
haphazardly unpicking your work.

Suddenly everything *pigeon* has flown into
the net of your mind. No matter the glass or garden
separating you from them; you hear them purring
self-congratulatory as cats. A little engine's encased
in each muscular breast, like the pulse in your wrist.

Not long ago – *thud!* – a renegade interrupted your bed-making,
disturbed the dust on the pane, then fell back
onto the patio and exited this world. One less, you said,
though you waited for it to cool before bagging it up,
double-knotting the handles round its clawed feet.

You are no Darwin. You
watch obsessively; he obsessively watched
their habits & ways, and winced
as he laid his favourites down on the table
to administer the fatal dose of ether.

They gave him facts. He repaid them
with neat, handwritten labels
and preservation in a national museum.
But things were different back then.
You have no need for a theory of everything.

David Troupes

I'm fascinated by the dialogue that exists between a body and its setting, and most of my poetry grows from that feeling of expansion we get in large, unfettered places: a hill, a forest. These poems are all set in New England, either in my native Massachusetts or along the coast of Maine, where my wife and I lived for a short spell some years ago. I am of course (being a poet) hopelessly nostalgic, and poetry is a way for me to maintain a relationship with places I see too little of.

The final four poems are from *God of Corn*, a family or sequence I have been developing for several years. Each begins with a title, and in most cases a passage, from Josiah Gilbert Holland's 1855 book *A History of Western Massachusetts*. I approach these with a sense of drawing quickly, in large strokes, as with charcoal.

Indian Paintbrushes

The mouths are open—
the young tongues,

the soft teeth.
Old Lithuanians stand in their shirts by the onion tray.

Insects
gather to the lanterns,

the blue lawns are full of candles.
Pine-shadows

soothe themselves in pain.
Now our daughter

wakes
in her chair

and watches quietly the green berries. Up in the weeds
stars

eat each other like fish.
The east is dark, the west

full of bones and gowns.
By the bellows

of August
the bellows-men rest.

Swimming at Ovens Mouth

I

The sun and moon
dawdle in the evening crowns
as you open
your arms to the sharp water, the sky-colored knives.

II

The earth is round and we on the outside so everything spills
away, the tide's mind of eelgrass dwelling
on the deep from the shallows
where you dip over the silt and drift through the air with the
                                        sewing needles.

III

Periwinkle silence. Planets
flicker in the rafters.
You stand and wrap yourself in skin, in rivers and salts,
cooled, day-freckled for night.

IV

The earth is round and we on the inside so everything pools
to us, to our tent, bathed
in sea-smell and skin-smell,
a swamping-in of sleep, a warm flood of world floating our limbs.

The Vessel

Cold sun whiteness and sea-clover
and sun-pennies,
water-bowls drifting, water-hearts beating. We slide away

through the harbor, that tray of strange tools,
the sea
deepening beneath us. The rising

worsens, we are loosened, we race
through a bright
riot of flowers opening. The wind

hits us and lying on the deck is like standing
on the sea. The green hinters, the lucent gulls, the belfries
of cloud. What was that life? That cold salad dressed

in war, the ice water and lemon,
the air-conditioned foyers where the damned
empty their pockets. Patient tubers

of hate, winter squash of the heart. What news
came down the island's one wire
leached into the ground like profane medicine. Even the trees

were chin-deep in the world, they were drowning.
Those sluiceway
daisies, each bee the soft center

of its flower. And we now
at the tip of a tower in every direction, spattered
with jewels

and not one hand to a rope as we roll
and tack
in the teeth of innocence.

Echo Lake

The owl is a bell
for its pine,

making of that pine
a cathedral.

I recline
among the brown bones, January's bric–a–brac.

My meal is through and the smoke
from my snuffed fire

rolls
in a heavy blob over the reservoir

where winter
is founding ice upon the water, inching

its daggers, its ivy of light and dark.
Crows pass,

a slow communication.
White weeds grow upon the sun.

The owl removes itself
to another pine,

and makes
of that pine a cathedral.

Swimming the Deerfield at Stillwater

This water is not still: a dark glass
coiling with light, the mud–run
from an immaculate well, a wash of storm-spoil

sluicing July.
We arrive late, step down from the greenpapered walls
and sink our nails

among the squalls
of invertebrates flashing from the shallows. The bank drops,
the current takes us and we tip our heads

to face the long furl of late sky. Being in a river
makes everything a river. Evening
peels across the water: shelves of light,

canyons of light, weeping abrasions of light.
We sight the rocks, we muscle against the cold. The sea
wants us, it numbers us, even here, tangled

in the river a hundred miles inland,
treading the water-roots
as stars creep from their bushes over Greenfield,

over Turners Falls and Old Deerfield, among the trash of the eskers
and the pink-piled stones of the outcrops:
tangled with our wives and our husbands, fitting ourselves

to the river's sea-leaning repose,
all of us breathing with the river on our lips,
among the tips of sun, among the hills' faint alluvia.

Early Ascent of Mount Prospect from the Hopper

I

Corrugations of light and air. Dayfall glamor.
Hails and halos
of blue
over the majuscule of hills.

II

I climb into the sun—
the yellow stems, the manifold pins.
Ten years gone
and still the hills refine, the valley smoothes its linen.

III

Glutted by noon. For others I leave the decline—
parasol
of the outcrop pine.
I have my cup of sky, my mineral skin.

IV

This brook.
This ridge line of water, and the dark
pond its clouded peak.
For ten years the weather comes and goes, the hills clarify.

from God of Corn

During Those Long and Gloomy

During those long and gloomy years, the plough was often left to rot in the furrow, and faint and few were the encroachments made upon the forest. The fattest of the herd and the finest of the wheat were brought forth, too often without expectation of pecuniary recompense, to be sacrificed on the altar of political liberty.

The blood-brown scape
of another town lop-crossed
under low skies, the cold seethe
of another day in its begins—
farms circled
by the slabs of November. The world
is an engine of unmaking. In every vine-wall of knots
we recognize ourselves. Standing
in the mud yard we seem hardly to exist.
With only the nonsense games of children
we arrive at the gutted rabbit,
the ash-downed house. The meadow
clings soakingly with its soft teeth,
the sky
is a pail of cinders and—what is worse—a pail of cinders
is the sky.
In a swale of crabgrass waits the calf, eyes
lolling toward a vague middle distance
of vanished mother.
There is no weather coming which is not
already here, nothing new
under the vanished sun
as our daughters march to the well
to pull a day's water,
as our sons
war
crude shares into the earth. My own boy
is studying something he has found.
He looks at the earth. I watch him. I too
have a craft
to tack against the wind.

Mount Pomeroy and Mount Liza

*Mount Pomeroy and Mount Liza lift their peculiar conical forms, about a mile and
a half apart, each holding company with the tradition that gave it its name. Mount
Pomeroy received its name, it is said, from a combat which a man of that name had
with a bear upon its territory, and Mount Liza perpetuates a part of the name of
Elizabeth, the name of an Indian captive who was buried there.*

Gun in hand out the door and the raw
grows worse. The lessening
of November, the strick of wind
crowding and dividing the reeds. The town
passes quickly.
Into the woods now, where the trees are keys
all fitted to locks.
In a damp saddle between hills, among the hemlocks
are turkeys. Therefore the gun. Therefore
hope,
and the wincingness of sound.
Spent candles line the fir-sills.
We settle, a carcass
in repose, patient among the seeps
for our chance. We find mothers

in strange places,
and they raise strange sons. Rain
darkens the wood and glitters the fern.
Silence from the root-hovels.
The man who fought, the girl who died
are not a mind of light touching
hill to hill, are not
a weed flagging in the wet.
They are nowhere, are nothing.
Softly,
silently across the needles
turkeys roll their barrels of blood.
Our muscles tighten to our bones.
There is your mountain, son.
So climb.

And to Those Bleak Hills

Evening, and the world keeps trying to end. For the last
one thousand
seven hundred and fifty-five years the rivers
have been running,
lifting
the silt, cleaning the tubs
where the body bathes, weeding the white garden. In this
everything joins.
There are hands
taking up the seeds, sliding them from palm to pocket.
There are eyes casting about, a last counting.
Scent lingers by the scoured millwork.
Yet of myself
there is a scattering, of myself
the pieces fall, fissured
by sin and carried to the marsh.
The stones give their blood, the pond fills, the bluegills
break and breed.
When my brother's letter came
it was a relief to think
the worst had happened,
it was over—
had been over several days, even,
before I knew a thing.

The Allotments of Land Were Divided

The allotments of land were divided by lines running from the river to and upon the Hill, each containing a home-lot bordering the river, each a portion of the "hasseky marish," or meadow, lying between the home-lots and the hill, while the latter constituted the wood-lots.

The dry laurels and gnarls of sassafras
are a river flowing always
against us as we pass west, a torrent
of forest, up to our hips
in thorn, in whale-ribs of cedar. We are exhausted
of the forest and we owe it that.
Another hill rolls
slowly past us
like another wave past a piling.
The winter sun, the late weave
and the wind.
Our hands are flayed with cold.
So this is the valley—another lick
of the passing.
We see a pile of stumps, and a track
hurries us to the farms.
We see cattle, moon-oil in the dusk,
heads down, the high grass filling their ears.
We bite into the last
of our fruit, reminded
again how the skin
holds most of the flavor. Nearby
a fire ticks, giving
a weedling smoke, unbuoyant, a rumor
among the walls. And now a laugh
from boys at the end of their day, tending
the fire, watching the thorn go up.
A twilit weal, a salad of bitters.
Where the bound is sunk, there
this freedom ends. Yet the man we are
so desires the farm
as he walks by, walking late—
wants to jump the fence, join

the fire, stand
in the crowd of the fire
and be a part
of that burning, a part of that having.

Ben Rogers

Many of the poems here began from some sort of impulse to write about a specific thing or image, and then to discover through writing where this impulse would lead. Discovering and following a path or paths is a recurrent focus in these poems, whether it be describing routes that are so personal that no objective mapping system could possibly chronicle them in 'The Ways Forward', or charting different movements in and around the convoluted 'Vogue Gyratory'. As well as literal journeys there are journeys created through internal narratives, such as in 'Mackerel Salad' or 'Monstera Deliciosa/Semantic Satiation', which can have an escapist function though can also generate additional levels of disorientation, a kind of mental labyrinth. Thoreau once said that 'Not until we are lost do we begin to understand ourselves', and I am interested in exploring the drama that can exist in being lost as well as the freedom of it.

Moon Jellyfish

Is the name given to thoughts, fat and changeable,
that have a kind of aloof machinery to them. You,

by which I mean you not everyone, might be indifferent
to the idea of someone attempting to articulate the feeling

they get when they sense their shadow is somehow
held up, as though a tendril of it has been caught

in a door that was closed too quickly, or maybe
compromised by the complicated silhouette of a cloud

that's got jammed in the sky by a sluggish
wind. Your indifference, by no stretch a deep-down

feeling, is a small organism, perhaps scooped into
existence by someone's interrogative glance that

felt in a way parental, and has a thin membrane
to it that means it could easily jumble into any number

of other drifting dispositions. When you look at it
though, twisting slowly in a syrup of midnight, you

cannot not consider how easily aesthetics, by trumping
all else, can become the slinkiest of anaesthetics, although

in thinking that you're also aware that, if someone
held a lamp over you, four squat bulbs flooding

your head from crown to collar, you wouldn't stake
your life on it. You wouldn't stake anything on it.

Vogue Gyratory

How the present complicated system offers any advantages is beyond easy
comprehension. It makes one wonder if the planner responsible was power mad...
                                                          – *Brighton Bits* blog post

a

An unseen voice concludes *progress is progress.*
When passing, sometimes there's the dilemma
between the two adjacent crematoria, the one further
up the hill or the one nearer its foot. One has a better
view, the other is less effort, though both criteria
are arguably redundant. At the base of the hill,
the gyratory, a washing machine of cars in the middle
of which is a man washing his car, a brushed aqua
Yaris. The sun sliced by chimneys, a dying head-
lamp. The phrase hasn't been updated yet.

b

No glamour about the latest gull's performance
singing its throat out from the ridge of *The Bear*
Inn before crafting a series of improvised
swerves and dives towards the marina. The sun
has mutated into a mandarin that's been kicked in the gut.
You can't, unless a machine, draw perfect circles.
The clock that used to watch over a factory line's
spool of pills now points down on a five-bagged woman U-
turning back into Sainsbury's to collect the local paper
telling her that the big wheel might be chopped.

c

Past last orders and the car lights are six-point stars
that zip round a circuit not unlike a waltzer. The shape
is perhaps akin to an amoeba, a supposedly simple
organism. You might ask it the question *Why do*

you make life so complicated? and it might, as you did,
find the word *so* a cruel emphasis, and wonder what
else it could have done. Maybe it would respond
by saying simplicity isn't exactly in fashion.
A man steps up to draw cash from its heart
so he has the requisite fuel to drive round it again.

The Vogue Gyratory is a traffic junction in the city of Brighton & Hove.

Mackerel Salad

Turned left out of the room, and returned for the security pass.
Conversation about pass, do you need it to get out.
Should it be possible for a building to require you to need a pass
    to get out.
Pressed button to get into stairwell and then because the light
    was flashing alternate green and orange you didn't need the
    pass to get out.
Turned right out of the building, many going the opposite way,
    and while doing so planned to get mackerel salad.
Crossed the road to a traffic island, thought about the odds of
    getting hit by a truck.
Odds increase of getting hit if you're thinking about something
    else while crossing, including thinking about the odds of
    getting hit.
Crossed the road from traffic island to other pavement, saw an
    advertisement for mortgages.
Pros for mortgages: the image of yellow flowers on a wooden
    countertop. Cons for mortgages: the word *mort* means
    death and *gage* means count.
Momentary contemplation about the countdown to death while
    passing a man with dice on his tie.
Entered the usual café and bought the mackerel salad, served by
    a woman with glasses who didn't quite make eye contact
    while smiling so was actually smiling at some air space.

Took the mackerel salad to a square in front of a church, thought
about wavering prayer and murmuring candles.

Consideration of the paving arranged in circular patterns.

Started to pace round the square following the circular patterns,
stepping on the individual paving slabs and not touching
cracks.

Are they assembled to cater for some sort of ritual.

Do they reflect some sort of astral cartography.

How did Pluto feel when it was told it was not a planet.

Pluto doesn't feel things, because it's elemental.

Thought that it's hard to know that for absolutely sure.

Decided to ring a friend, and it went straight to answerphone, a
recorded woman's voice neither of us know.

Didn't leave a message because of having heard sound of own
voice on previous occasion and it sounding like someone
else.

On that basis you might not speak at all.

Decided on a bench, sat on the right hand side nearer the coffee
stall and ate first fork of mackerel salad.

Man at the coffee stall recommends the white chocolate and
cherry flapjack to a woman in a dark red coat, but she
doesn't buy it.

Thought about the different reds, thought about predators in
fairy tale.

Read on phone an old post from days ago about someone giving
up using their phone for the day the next day, although
they will still use the internet.

Thought about being in a wilderness where phones won't work.

The wilderness had parched olive trees and powdery dirt, as well
as stagnant water and reeds nearby to the right and up a
narrow path, if you can call it that, on the left.

The woman said earlier that this was the last day of the salad.

Thought that some last days go without you noticing, is it better
if you notice. Recalled the air conditioning unit in gated
car park of a building south-west from the square towards
the river, how when passing it it used to have a ticking
sound that created the sense time was running out.

The last few times it has stopped ticking.

The sky isn't a mackerel one because the clouds are too large.

The wind can't decide where it's going.

Monstera Deliciosa/Semantic Satiation

The sort of plant someone might grip a name on, a name
lodged on a bath's corner ledge. A trickle from the pot,
shot with loam. Each leaf is an open hand with gaps
between the fingers, which imply a loose hold on money,
and which could connect to having a blank with names.
A name that doesn't make you think of cheese. The plant
is a disorder that hangs over you, a shadow over a sheet
of water you cannot name, a shade you associate with
the metallic weight of regret. In the mirror, your face
has a tug to it you don't want to name. There's a folly
to the multi-feather-duster effect that the fronds have
as your father parades the plant down the hall on a plate
whose pattern you don't have the wherewithal to name.
The plant has achieved a size where it can no longer perch
and has been delivered to a new home behind the television,
there being no name like home. The television is in the room
named the living room, to distinguish it from the other
rooms. The fire reaches out to feather the guard. If the fire
were solid you'd name it a bed of thorns. Your mother
prods for a new channel, but before she does the news
broadcaster with a name you can't name announces
the death of a name you can't name who appeared in a show
with a name you can't name. The leaves reach out to smother
the television. The carpet's name is soft earth, the wallpaper's
name is mountain slate, the ceiling's name is a heart turned
to ice. The next trivia question in order to win a slice
named a cheese is to name the plant in the corner. Another
time, the plant there will be named a Norwegian spruce.
The window's names are outside, reality, growing up
and danger. This time though, the plant is unnameable.
Your parents have left the room, and you are left on the sofa
with your name, a word that reflects you but you see
through. A glass word and a plant that can't nurse. You imagine
the plant will move again, and in years to come will plunge
its many feet into hills spun with pine and flint. Returning
again to your name, it's not your name any more, and doesn't
even taste like a name, let alone name like a name.

Exeunt

Returning from the bathroom, he finds the lounge freshly vacant,
still warm with *bonhomie*: a small pyramid of cigarette ash settling
itself in a geometric cut-glass dish, flutes of cherry prosecco
birthing bubbles, a wipe of candy lipstick shining on the rim
of one, a bent-back paperback breathing itself into shape again,
the partition into the dining room sticky with fingerprints
at thigh-height of chocolate parfait, a demure berg of cork bobbing
in a half-drunk merlot, an errant faux-pearl button upturned
and winkled behind the ankle of the taupe newly upholstered
armchair. The talk of how much the chair cost yet hangs
in the air, along with the comment of the woman from down
the road that his responses were *most salient*, a mere moment
before he'd excused himself to then wonder, while he relieved
himself, while he glanced at the smiling family trio snapped
and clip-framed on a plane of damp sand, what she meant by *salient*.
He now sits on the edge of the ruby chaise longue, watches
the television mutely pedal down the closing minutes of the year,
the silent fireworks spraying over the city, bouquets of unsmellable
colour, the camera panning slowly over a dark ocean of faces
he doesn't know, as they traipse through a song they don't know.

Searching for a Woman in Fes

That way. He takes the coin, returns to dice
and I follow the trace of his finger through

a large arch, a yawn of blue and gold, down
streets cut like rivers, so old they've dropped

names, stamped out by the heavy tread of mules.
I know you're here. Children scatter like seeds,

little puffs of spice, one stepping up,
chiming out *chips and gravy, chips and gravy,*

as though imaginary food will solace the lost.
He leads me (not for free) down gaunt alleys,

where walls lean in, shedding scorched skin
and then he's gone, just dust, orange peel, the wail

of fourth prayer. I pass stalls sloped with garlic,
coils of fabric, the odd head of camel, to reach

a chair, feeling steam melt from sticky mint tea,
the out-of-tune fuzz of a television fizz on my ear

and watching the hand of a man playing dominoes,
tapping his temple as he stubs out a dead end.

Sheherazade

I draw curtains, light lamps as he, humped
like an ape, gapes at a leopard prowling
in plasma. The powdery eyes of its fur
blur as it hurls at its prey. She gets away.

He swigs, I switch channel. Prison romance,
D-list dance, talk-show threesomes, real-life
crime. That makes his feet twitch – a girl's
chunked remains unwrapped from a ditch.

With that gory story I serve his steak
and kidney, a clutch of chips. As he punctures
the pie, brown mince laps the plate,
I ponder *his* insides, what colour they take.

We tread up to bed. *Listen to this* I say,
on two men tripping down steps at work.
One even broke his back. *I hope he was black*,
he mutters, his rump thumping the banisters.

As we enter the room, I gabble on spiders,
snakes, lakes of jewelled fish. He stares, waits
while my words burn, sand filling my throat.
Dumb. Then he yanks blinds, thumps lights,

slams me, rams me down. But I am gone.
I gallop on cloud, while Earth crawls below,
a drop, a clod. I am meteor blazing in space.
I sail the nebula of night.

And when my bed lands, my husband sleeps,
a deep furrow of snore. His right hand trails
the carpet on the floor, a loose strand
I'll sew tomorrow.

A Space Azalea

*This azalea sprouted out from a seed of azaleas that had travelled in space with
a medical doctor and the first Japanese woman who had explored space.*
           – sign in courtyard of Matsumoto Castle

The absence of things, a plant shedding

a scattered signature of red. The name –
        something about remembering home.

In embryo, it had sensed its planet,

a dot smeared on a vast plane, the patch
        of crust where, free

from spinning in the frameless dark,

it would land, reconstitute and grow,
        unbend its stalk, start pandering to the sun,

set root. It's an *a*, not a *the*, other

pieces may be elsewhere, outside
        this immurement, walls famed

for their blackness. Black in the way space is not.

The Ways Forward

From charred wood on the rock–garbed beach
to the path that zags the hill recently combed
with rain. *An oscillation, a sharp jerk*
to the left, lurch sunbound, then swipe up
as though striking something out.

From back round the corner by the cobbled
wall to the quacking pond beset with willow.
A hurtle forward then off-kilter as if tripped,
a wild jungled motion calming to a loose
scribble, then a u-turn to find the culprit.

From mist–coloured pillars scrapped by time
to the crumbling sentence of a staircase's
foot set upon by sea. *An un-hooking*
clockwise, reverse meander, impulsive
curl, then rat-a-tat tumble to abrupt standstill.

From the weedy pavement of a suburban street
whose name can't be remembered to a tiled
porch washed with ochre light. *A whiplash*
initially towards NNW, then a flux of motion
in a confined space, aping a brain-duff moth.

From the thick of a long backlog of pines
engulfed in syrupy dusk to the lone car
waiting at the edge of the lake. *A scattergun
straight ahead, followed by downward stabs
right in fast-improvised sweeps.*

From click-clacking escalator that you no longer
stand on to the seat you've forgotten at the front
of the top-deck. *An acute-angled chicane,
undulation as of missed wingbeat, tightrope
move to 9 o'clock, crotchet rest, zoomed chuck.*

Tom Docherty

The thoughts of José Ortega y Gasset on translation are significant to the way I think about speech in general, and poetry in particular. To say something is already a translation of thought, but sometimes when it is said it seems to be other than the thought. The shape and sound of the word is its own kind of thought. Man's inevitable privilege, according to Ortega y Gasset, is 'never to achieve what he proposes, and to remain merely an intention, a living utopia'. These poems, then, fail in what they intend, but I hope their intentions themselves are not failures. I think poetry is not simply 'memorable speech' but an attempt at speech outside speech: both below and beyond it. Perhaps that is why these poems turn to music, architecture, the mathematics of both. The words are going all *out*, in various modes, to add up to more than they are.

Theory of Tuning Pianos

It begins not with a book
nor even an attentive ear.
You have to sit and live with the thing.
You must learn to see grand gestures
in a shiver, discern
each silence of every different moment.

Now place a finger. Be careful:
you are pressing on a beating heart.
Desire to understand nothing that is not
this beating heart. You cannot hear
the equations being made
perfect between two bodies.

Sound in another place. It is yours
to say well- or ill-tempered. Align shoulder
and breast. When time for movement,
move; rest
in the intervals. If your touch is not light,
make light of your thought.

So much is said by the breath
that follows. You are now
at the heart of the way
all this is numbered.
It is imperative you do not speak.
It begins to sound like your lover is awake.

At the Grave of Ludwig Wittgenstein

Not death but overgrowth. Gorgeous
throat of earth, excess of abyss:
I see the stumps of trees and raise
them the constellation-branches,
a second nature's necklaces,
and this, a string of sentences
but not. This strings what I invent.
I have no idea where you went.

On Gaudí's Geometry

Articulate
the governances
of a leaf:
where light,
where water

ribs of xylem
and of phloem's flow
vault the thing,
map it.
The body

communicates.
No drop, no blood cell
stops pool-still
in such
flush-angled

capillaries.

Vespertine Colloquium with a Soldier of the Holy Roman Empire

Well of course the *imperium* will implode!

It teaches rebellion by conquest! We start in blood and botulism
   but we end in books. Pinakes and ciboria sprout
   from Aachen to Saint-Denis; we make bedposts
   for love's sacrifice. Misericords
   relieve us, first *in ecclesiam*, then of our enemies *in agro*.

Barbaric? You mean foreign. To conquer with order
   is a gift. The genitive belongs to you now.
   Here are our cases, where
   do you keep the drink? You can have no picture
   without a frame — ours (it's plique-à-jour).

Long live Charlemagne and Charles Martel's mantle.

The Königspfalzten cry out *Pater Europae* (not
   quite a paternoster); crepuscular
   rays reach the emperor's robes.

Alcuin's mind is English and delectable: *vox populi*, he knows,
   is Christendom by morning and whoredom
   by mid-afternoon. But Eriugena's brain is Irish
   porridge, not worth its salt or salary.

What I take is what a lover takes. The soldier's pay
   is a warm reception. The poet says
   nos quoque per totum pariter cantabimur orbem
   iunctaque semper erunt nomina nostra tuis
   — yes, even your names for yourselves
   will be entwined with ours, even
   the raindrop names in night's parched vale (*vale*).
   You will be sung *sub voce*, a few cents
   under our tongues.

But at *Completorium*, remember these are interludes.
        I saw a thousand men fall at my side,
        and ten thousand more at my right hand.
        They will not be remembered.
        I am trying to give, not to take. These few valiant
        are tympana, archivolts for the *tabernaculum*,
        where the building is not my notion or yours.

What did he say? *glorificabo*. Come on in.

Poem after a Funeral

Rhotic tremble
of a bee

in the garden's last
summer wind:

I tell it
of an old family friend

who also
swallowed spring.

The Herbs of Scotland

O herb of Scotland!
I have not yet smelt you properly,
nor eaten of you, nor felt I could use you
even to heal the odd midgie-bite.
It is time now to take my country
by the throat, or by the heart,
by rambling through sweet meadows for meadowsweet,
by netting nettles for their metal-strong soup,
by bottling blaeberries (which are not blueberries
but Scots for bilberries) thatched in heather
during the winter. O beautiful unbarren blue land!
St John's Wort, ugly on its English face,
is a beauty spot, a word-painting round these parts —
achlasan Chaluim Chille — Columba's oxterful —
the herb a saint gave
to a cattle-boy as proto-Prozac, hugged
into the blood, to calm his fear
of cold cow'rin nights and cold cows' eyes...

> *Buainidh mi mo choinneachan,*
> *Mar choinneamh ri mo naomh,*
> *Chasga fuath nam fear foille,*
>   *Agus boile name ban baoth.*

I will string you, I will sing you along, Scotland
through Scotland, though you will not know, *mo caraid*,
mo bhilis, mo gradh, will steam the scent of you
from myrrh, to keep the heart from withering,
will use your yarrow to bleed a hard head,
and rest in your heather bed until you decide
that you kissed me among the reeds
because you wanted me to eat of you, you wanted me
to press you hard enough to share
in your billowing bloodstream.
Then I will pick mountain willow, which, even under snow-screen,
nestled in an unknown pillow,
blooms.

Spes Scotorum

after Adomnán

I. A Visitation

MY DRUID was Christ the Son of God. Loved of the Erin Twelve, I sailed to the salt-main on which the sea-gulls cry, one grey eye looking back to my little Oak Grove.

After the psalter-battle they sent me on my coracle. So many men dead for some strokes of a pen, they said. I kept at my work without compulsion, keeled onto this rock, this Alba. Ravens stretched over brine.

As a child my fellows were the badger and the pine marten. Yes, I made water wine, but that was an old trick then; I preferred picking weeds and thinking at times of time's beauty and the most naked body.

Back then, fussing with my playthings, I blinked and winds contrary turned favourable. Look around: you are making nothing move. Pitiful snoring beast, this is your hour to love.

II. The Dove's Hymn

We____ the un – mý_–_ sti – cal have ré_–_____ course to__ you

whose name_____is grea_–_____ter than much_____

ri_–____ chès. You who bróught___ the milk_–_____ skin

báck____from êbb-tide,_____kéep_____a_–__way

the waves_____

_____from this____sà_–____lty____léaf.

To My Twin in the Womb

You face away from me in the sailing bed
Cut granite stays course
The rain follows me uphill
Flowers examine the field

We are made in water we are made
To feel we are not made to exist
Ranunculus abortivus
I daresay I will wait here awhile

The Last Point of Sight

Yes, only one star is visibly here
tonight and yes, it is saying
then, then, then like a white dog
and it is saying *before you were born,*
saying *I was before you were born,*
before you or any of this was thrown
knock-kneed into a struggle for breath, I was
and you do not know if I am anymore,
wild grasses along the roadside
are nodding heavily in sad, old-man agreement,
every little blade visibly agreeing,
though at different times, and in varying frequencies
according to the heft of each single heave;
and yes — continuing from my street
along and slowly down the blue-black oak hill
and over the stone bridge over a pebble burn
to the next family of lights —
the end of the fencepost trail
and the end of the line of the curves
are always evading the last point of sight,
which appears to say
continue, to say

follow like a dog or a man
led by a dog, since you do not know where you are anymore;
and yes, okay, the star is even blinking now leg-tremblingly
as if it was a shivering old man before there were old men,
to nail its point into the sky,
to repeat for now and tonight the word *fragility*,
appearing to curve a visibly broken line

and yet all that travels beyond it is now
will we continue to love
though we remain
heaved and blind and not yet born.

Centoum

from Les Murray

I walk on home where the stars are thinnest, glancing
the dented light of milk cans.
I will wake up in a world that hooves have led to
the edge of dark country. I could not afford

the dented light of milk cans
in winecellar towns at peace with their horizons.
The edge of dark country I could not afford
hangs over me moveless, pierced everywhere by sky.

In winecellar towns at peace with their horizons,
the tree grows troubled, trembles, shifts. Its crown
hangs over me moveless, pierced everywhere by sky.
On a landscape wide as all forgiveness

the tree grows, troubled, trembles, shifts its crown.
I walk on home where the stars are thinnest, glancing
on a landscape wide as all forgiveness.
I will wake up in a world that hooves have led to.

Molly Vogel

These poems are multilingual, exposing an amalgam of poetic cultures (Scottish, for one) as a byproduct of inhabiting a new country, while keeping the old. As a garden is varied, so are the poems. Many of the poems are ekphrastic, in direct conversation with art as nature, nature as art. The idea is to make of each budding poem a collective garden. Traditionally, Japanese floral arranging is done in silence. The stem and leaves are composed, drawing emphasis toward shape, line, frame. I often think about arrangements in the way that I think about Kanji characters: pictorial, compressed, understated. One stroke becomes part of a greater whole. The condensation of the objective and the direct in floral arranging and poetry intensifies the sense of beauty in a single flower, or word, similar to the Imagists' idea of isolating objects through the use of 'luminous details'.

Interruption and Completion of a Thought

In class, the shared-desk, you are next

to me. I am trying to think

of the last line to a haiku:

black hair

kuro kami no

tangled in a thousand strands

chisuji no kami no

tangled my hair and

midaregami

tangled my tangled memories

omoi midare katsu

My love

we wade into holiness

wait in loneliness

the weight-stone of blessed duress.

Stillness: a single finger slips down the neck

of my boot, and still—

our long nights of love-making

omoi midaruru.

Glasgow Haiku

I

after Bashō

auld dub—
a puddock plops
tae wade the watter

II

the ither night
anely hoffway hame
doon it came all
plump like.
jus pissn.
an nae coat.
jist shows ye disnit,
jist goes tae show ye.

The Child Dreaming in a Poet's House

after Seferis

The flowering dark and the ravine which holds the moon waning
the papery lids close to the north wind like confetti and the wind
poppy vellum is skin between pages of a book; the stars are the sails of some
lost person. On the bedside sits the rind of the satsuma.

I have bridled my whole heart, a golden bit among apple orchards
on holy grass sweet the tall hierochloe is a bride, white throats pushing
up from wet stones in mud; dawn has two faces.
I have bridled my whole heart, on your left thigh a mark,
a basin creek at your knee, I have seen the long way your body
comes in from the rain, a great stone in bed, perhaps you exist
best sitting on a picket fence, a long line.

The face I see does not ask questions nor does the boy
watching from a distance. I climb the fence; I hold all of summer
in my hands. Beneath me the great body is flanked by bare feet,
no skein of rope. Into the distance I am gone with no line. The wheat
field folds over in my memory. Only fire on the peaks; they ask nothing
neither time a window frame nor sound. I have bridled my whole heart
on the silence of entire air. I don't have to speak.

I close my eyes to find the secret meeting place
under the breathing of the coast live oak
the tall grass against itself sounds like human voices
like the memory of your voice saying is there anything as still
as sleeping horses, there where the star lilies end, however hard
you try to recall your childhood years, however much you've asked
bodies to stay awhile under the blanched tree
branches way out in the plain, where a run of the sun,
naked, stood still, and not a sound was made and your heart
shuddered, I close my eyes; I have bridled my whole heart.

Yesterday's rain
and the water still in hoof prints.

On Heidegger's *Being and Time*

I

When I was fourteen, I wanted to play the violin. I did not
have the discipline of my twin, her feet
dragging before her eyes down each stair early
before seminary each morning. My Mom accompanied her
on the piano, a remnant from girlhood that came before
books and boys. Vanessa played while she thought
and Mom thought I slept upstairs.
I was listening: a book by my bedside and my black lab asleep
in my twin bed.

Now, I would hear Mother say. It is time, *now* is the time. Everyone
is waiting for you. Your siblings are waiting for you
in the car. God is waiting for you, too.

II

The metronome tsks time. It is telling the *now*,
now, *now*, *now*. It is the quiet from the before,
the clamor of what is to come: four equally stressed
sixteenths. The details deliberate, the need for discipline
in the disparate. The phrasing of time being
robbed from one note to another. Refuge in order:
the absoluteness of a thing holding time, holding time
in time. Pointing to *now*, no, *now*—though the tick–tick sound
has come and gone before it has come.

III

Listen: one can only wait
for nothing; nothing waits
for no one. I know nothing,
know no end

Flora and Fauna

I

on highway seventeen to the northeast
side of aptos toward soquel
there meets two creeks
sempervirens falls
into big-basin near
the chaparral pea

II

i am thinking your body could be
california: it is the same sharp-shinned
hawk your mouth red huckleberries
            your hair feathers
            on the dark-eyed junco
            quietly in the redwood tree

III

wild (at our first) beasts words
—our coming makes stones sing like birds—
but o the starhushed silence which ours thirsts
            you and i in my thinnest dress
            the root-knot path
            in green chinquapin thirds

IV

let us lurch and press in the woods
and i will make a dress of your words—
red-wood violet, little trillium, my mountain iris
            speak to me the costanoan language
            make me your *mukurma* woman
            sii water taste me like *oo'-rahk* salmon

V

a would-home of knob-cone
pines my love (cheeks flush
like bush poppies)

Colloquy with a Closed Window

The sun is God.
— J.M.W. Turner

I   In my lap   a closed *Harmonium*. Its yellowed jacket
         recalls butter-milk poppies. Covered in a funeral
procession of words, it could be a publisher's last memo. My bedfellow
for three days   I carry it with me in the space of Santa Cruz: hyperion
tree, to Mass (no accident!); I've been taking it to the zoo (to get acquainted),
and—finally—I wake with the first sun   in my eyes, it
      lying open   on my chest.

Thanks to an age-old jealousy, an inability to love in twos,
                          I lightly doggy-ear
         a page (or two): 'I am content when wakened birds,
before
they fly, test the reality
of misty fields, by their sweet questionings.'   A nod
          and a page or two fleeting encounters.

II   As much a book of silences as chirpings.

III   The first I could do when I swallowed it whole was take a long
         nap. I was caught in amber   as captured light.
Light: the whole sky onto my head, a blue sets blue round, down onto
                           the naked
      backs of tops.

I listen for an answer: look at the lilacs.   From a distance his page looks
         blank: empty space. (No need to worry.) He is all   wide
                                            open, a door   off its hinges.
            Step into the lightening
      and a bird becomes the only exhalation: 'when the blackbird flew out
                                                                    of sight,
      it marked the edge' (the edge)
                                'of one   of many circles.'
                        A radiant weight.

IV   Light. On one
                        side of a line. In true fashion: 'an up and down
between two elements
a fluctuating between sun and moon.'
                        Chiaroscuro
      all bottled up in a jar: the jar of every day, the jarring everyday.
                                I fling open   the book: refracting light.
            An alchemist: 'the spring is like a belle undressing.'
Further, farther: 'the gold tree is blue, the singer has pulled his cloak
over his head. The moon
        is in the folds of the cloak.'

V   blue: imagination
                        tawny: reality
                        green: body
                        aureolin: sun
                        taupe: mirth

            furniture for the page.

VI   A simple matter of trust: what is written is life. You can't avoid it.

Glesga Prayer

Our Father who art in heaven, I am in love.
Again. For which I offer thanks.
Tonight, I step in dog shit. I don't care.
I thank God for it. I ought to start with praise,
but praise is hard for me. Did I tell you
about the boy who taught me how to pray?
He always starts with praise. I see him from time
to time. Do you? Once at the train station
I said I want to have dinner with you. He said I want to eat
with you, I want to eat on you, I want to eat you!
Take care of him.

Now, confession—the worst part. At night
the fox crosses the street to eat from a bin.
He looks like a tired-faced woman except
he is beautiful. I'm sorry for the times I've stayed
out in short long rain. Soft with dew, I look
like a small puddle. And in my loneliness and fear
I've thought create in me a clean heart O God.
Forgive me. This is my favorite sin: despair—
whose lust I celebrate with love and prayer.

Heavenly Father, thank you for this greasy, delicious
mince pie and this fish supper (though
it's made me kind of sick). Also thanks
for this Irn-Bru, so sweet and so cold.
At the gardens last week, I sat and watched
two boys blowing up johnnies. I could have
let it mean anything but was moved again
by how little we ask for. Two mums pushed
their children in the opposite direction.
I laughed and got a dirty look. Dear Lord,
we move with love from metaphor to metaphor,
which is—let it be so—a kind of prayer.

I'm usually asleep by now. I won't bother you
with requests. Though keep the one I love safe.
Perhaps even a little bit of money my way…

This city is perched on the skyline like dirty doves.
It makes me think sometimes of you. What makes me
think of me is the poor soul who swims out
too far and then looks back to land. Ahead, he sees
eternity, and suddenly his arms no longer work,
and down he goes. As I fall fast, remember me.

Lessons on How to Understand a Famous Painting

Self-Portrait, Albrecht Dürer

I. In this canvas, people have seen their husband, an accurate depiction
of the Flemish people, a portrait of Martin Luther disguised as Albrecht
Dürer, a coat I am intentionally wearing so I can comment aloud to
others viewing the painting that I am wearing a similar coat to the one
in the painting, or a vermillion ore that is found only in the nether
regions of Madagascar which, when exposed to mercury, disintegrates
into a million pieces, giving the artist the exact shade of green desired.

II. In only very rare circumstances has the painter been able to refer so
deliberately to himself. Missing from the canvas is the mirror into which
the artist gazes: half of it displays the artist adjusting his moustache, the
other his non-existent trousers. His reflection does not surprise him; he
has seen it many times and, in fact, likes it; but he is badly painted and
reminds one of stale coffee, or a bad photograph of oneself that cannot
be forgotten.

III. The methodical chestnut strokes filling the background have been
frequently compared to chocolate, or the chattering leaves of fall. The
truffle, a German delicacy, if eaten, would have killed him. How often
Albrecht Dürer painted his own curls and felt the curve of the brush
between his fingers, bending and aching quietly like a piano bench, or
a creased page in a book. But it was already too late and the hair was
finished. Albrecht knew it and sensed it was a terrible mistake.

IV. Step away from the canvas and this man is staring right at you. Take ten steps back and he appears familiar, as if you saw him once, but aren't sure where. Look closely. It appears he has written, 'It is fitting that a liar should be a man of good memory.' It might be the Devil who is saying these words and maybe you believe them because they are being spoken by a man who looks like Jesus.

Lot's Wife

after Szymborska

Memory has what it sought.
It is customary to hear her breathe
the breath of Jehovah.

He has already forgotten
his neck does not feel
many-eyed fear.

For want of eternity ten thousand
grains have been composed.
She has the look of one just born.

Her eyes might be open.
The salt-crown has outlasted the head.
She is not a statue, but a mound.

If anyone had seen her,
they might have thought her holy.
One breath—she is gone.

Danaë

Gustav Klimt, 1907

It's been
thousands
upon thousands
of years of gold.
I was a god,
and this is what I did,
striking
without hands,
or hammer,
piercing
without needle,
without tools other
than gold,
gold,
the color gold.

Isle of Skye

I wanted to know where love comes from
without you in the world, I am drowning
through the port at Mallaig, across thirty acres
of heathered heath, the old northeast glebe
keep my pockets full of flowers.
And then I remember: it is you
I miss in the fetterless body
of every living name: bluebell,
bog myrtle, yellow rattle,
thistle. You are every shade
of twayblade, root, and twinflower.
When love is not enough,
what is left but primrose, bearberry,
the weightless crux of water lily?

The yew yawns a psalm.
The rood-bloom bows.
Tell me our story with/out
referent, with half-moon reverence.
I want to tell you what I couldn't say
most nights, take my hand along the edge
of it all is no line, only fond
foolishness, how I love the seriousness
of your fingers and the way you word
my half-name like amen. I stand
between white-beam and beech
like men. Where is my compass rose
amongst the rose garden?
Give all my longing to the River Brittle
down in the valley. There is no wait
in a flower, the too-late bower.

The Loves of Plants

I don't remember my first brush with pollen, yet I've watched words
flower sideways across your mouth.

– Elizabeth Willis

These stems are trembling, I pluck them
up. I have /ˈdʌbəlju:/'s rattling
in my mouth. The wind is
what caused them to bloom
a forsaken flower, the blood
of its dead lover. They cling too
closely to my tongue, stammering the stem
of the thing. The word is clanking:
anemone, anemone, anemone.

Joey Connolly

A poet I admire wrote recently – being (slightly) disparaging about my poems – 'I can respect a radical distrust of language, but it leaves me asking the question – so what are you going to do about it?' Which might turn out to be making a valid criticism; at the very least it touches on something I think about a lot. Or something that the narrators of my poems think about a lot (which admittedly doesn't make them the kind of people you'd want to get stuck talking to at a party). Nearly all of the poems here seem to be narrated by someone who wants to say something ostensibly very simple ('I'm sad about this' or 'The seaside is nice'), but who ends up getting caught up in the complexities of the act of communication itself. So a distrust of language certainly wasn't meant to be the *subject* of the poems. But philosophising and rationality and wordiness seem to me to be usually masking – and therefore implying – some much more sappy, sentimental thing, in a strange reflection of the way that simple emotional statements actually hold the enormous complexity of any specific instant, which the currents of our culture, history and all our washy psychology bind up in it. Does that answer the question 'so what are you going to do about it?' Oh, I guess not. Damn. I'm sad about this. The seaside is nice.

What You've Done

i.m. Rachel Jardine

or one thing you've done: thrown yourself
more hugely amongst
my neat web of signification, so that
ballet comes with a picture of you tacked to it,
so that *Sartre* has your scar by its
right eyebrow, and *jumper* your crazy smile,
and *blue* your birdlike nerves, your neatness,
the neat math of your thoughts, your thoughts.

And *bloom*, after the car-park of Bloom St., puts you
somewhere before Joyce's Bloom, but after –
even still – after a picture of an unnamed orange flower
from a textbook, under the German for *flower*. There's really
no connection   the net of implication
like everything comes apart in your hands.

Poem In Which Go I

There but for the conciliatory haze of fiction go I.
There but for the crazy kindness of strangers
go our crises of identity. There
but for the salt wind off the sea
goes the gold-drenched memory of 1992's
family holiday. There but for the graze of fog go we.

There but for the winnowing of Yahweh
go so many of our quaintest folk-statuettes. There
but for the faintest sense of justice
goes the conciliatory haze of fiction. There but for the
uncomfortable persistence of humanity
goes the neighbourhood.

There but for the harrowing frequency of laundry-days
goes the grace of God. There but for the slough of despond
goes our Christian. There but for one specific curtain of
palm-fronds goes the amber clarity of our faith.

There but for the goes of going walks our lord. There
but for the gauze of saying so goes all.

Your Room at Midnight was Suddenly

after Cavafy, 'The God Abandons Antony'

I

rich with the feeling of your hearing
an unseen procession, a procession rich itself
with the strains of its beauty, a low
darkness of voices – but now
is no time to mourn your loss,
your departing fortune – a life's work
spoiling before your eyes, a host of plans
proving illusory. As if you were
prepared, ever (as if you were brave),
say farewell to the Alexandria that is leaving.

And further: do not allow yourself
the lie of having dreamt, that your ears fail,
or your draining mind. Do not sully this
moment's song with the baseness of your desire
for stability. But as if

you were prepared, ever –
as if you were brave – move,
steady, to the window, as one
given for a city such as this,
this hugeness, move to the window and
beat with the pulse of feeling,
a feeling far off

from the pitched reed and entreaty of cowardice: no,
listen as a fatal delicacy to that voice,
that mass of beauty, that strange
and passing procession off
in the distant absence
of the Alexandria you are anyway losing.

II

on the table because god knows I'm no
romantic but I
                      want you. And underneath that
we sip our coffee and your eyes
are darker than any history or coffee, than any
Greek coffee ever was and hold the gloss
of immense depth only such darkness has. God knows
I want you to the point
of shucking the woman I love,
our house, the home we built
so slowly. And there is a procession offstage
which accompanies the upward swing
of your eyes, harmonises the argument
for discord, and you're explaining in an
almost unbroken English a poem from the Greek
of Cavafy: I don't know it. As if I were a coward

I keep quiet. On the table of my mind, I mean –
your room – hopeless
coward as I never thought
I was, hopeless neighbour of these
strains of romance language (the names
for your description, the country
my instinct will use to define you), close as I get
to the classicism of your Greek heart,
the close, Doric order of your form.
I don't know what it is which is leaving,
only the sweet draw of its
pain as it goes from me.

A Brief Glosa

I know that each one of us travels to love alone,
alone, to faith and to death.
I know. I've tried it. It doesn't help.
Let me come with you.

after Yannis Ritsos, 'Moonlight Sonata'

Twenty-four days, really, all told,
straggling Manchester's dive-bars until five for the pretext of drink
between the kitsch and neons as if there was no agony
keeping our bodies apart. Three-something weeks there, and then perhaps
three-thousand emails, Manchester to France. Praise be for smartphones.
I know that each one of us travels to love alone,

but this – this is surely unnecessary. By the time you left we'd settled
to a nightly routine: the Temple, the Thirsty Scholar,
the failing Black Dog Ballroom, always open, desperately, until dawn
with always a floor to ourselves. The cluttered inbox of lust
already blinking in my chest. And then we left,
alone, to faith and to death.

As in the time you took me back to the place you shared
with your absent fiancé to read me the Greek
of Yannis Ritsos, in Greek, until the sounds
worked by your tongue brought your tongue too much
into focus. Certain lusts can be swallowed, that noble, necessary gulp.
I know. I've tried it. It doesn't help.

Ritsos, with his *faith* and his *death*, is thinking more
of that intricate momentary balancing act, the fiddle of drink and time
by which we can hope to produce our presentable selves;
the phone screens and mildewed old editions
of the old translations you left me, all we believed we could afford
to eschew. Let me come with you.

That Rogue Longing

when it's otherwise all in order –
all settled, fine as alabaster – every feeling
accounted for, all told: it occurs

like a gnat which skips my swat –
chip of will – squat loaf
of matter – bold little exister.

Themselves

I have learned the words – curlicue,
arabesque, craquelure – and I have done my best
to feel that well-spoken weft &c. beneath

the skin of things, with ketamines or caffeines
mingling with the bloodstream I have long
been shifting, twice changing between Liverpool Street,

between St Pancras and here. All preparation
dissolves like cardboard minded
hangover morning vitamin supplement at this

sudden coast, the mist-hung edges of this shingle beach,
its pitchless singing, its pebble-rattle intensifying
to the static hiss of unthinkable numbers, this

vast variegate of stone being
dragged across itself by the persistent
knowing drugged retreat

of the waves, and the gentle waves – patina, spindrift,
astringent – and the waves. The vast multiplication table
of its rattle. The mingling of the symbols for stones

with the symbol for seawater rinsing the two,
the three-inch give of a tortoiseshell of shingle
underfoot, the way every rounded collateral pressure

of stone on deeper stone comes up
through the shoesoles, the soles of the feet,
up through some rail-cartographer's dream of nerves,

up to the neck and the graze there of the salt-air
on the tongue, scouring off the need for words
and, a breath after that, the words

The Finest Fire-Proofing We Have

It's a poem about a father insulating his family home,
written some time in 1924. It notices, the poem,
the knotted rope of his spine through his
flannel workshirt as he hunches to the skirting;
his intent fingers are working loose the dark wood,
panel by panel, and pressing in material from the roll of

asbestos matting behind him, before precisely
replacing the board. With aching thumbs he rocks its nails
back into their beds, as the poem settles its nouns into their gullies,
investing itself as fully as it can in how unflinchingly this father,
out of the dust of 1919, how fully this father surrounds with love his
young wife, their new son. It drags and it dwells on this love,

it weeps for it, almost, this love inhabiting 1919
and written of in 1924. There's love in the way panels are pried up
and replaced. And something else. How the poem's author, reading
of the Medical Board's classification of asbestosis
in 1925, how he was reminded of that young wife arriving home,
and the pride already metastasising inside the husband how

she'd never know how anything behind the boards had changed.

[untititled]

for AW

The orthodontic meddling of language
with the world, its snaggling malocclusions
between a group of objects and their name,

or the unnameable collusion of object and fact which
fritter truth like a spendthrift thrush
its energy in song. The determined unorthodoxy
in the solitary stance of a dock leaf, miles

from the nettles we suppose are its cause.
All I want is to tell you that I love you,
but true tessellation is a term from a diagram on your primary school

classroom wall. And the jaws have already sprung
closed over the moment, albeit gappily,
and I am stung into refuge among such

exquisite cosmetic meaninglessnesses as the
awkward stagger of a branch across the sky above me as it
divides the day's blue into jagged, arbitrary portions.

All I want is to propose that we be wrong
in corresponding ways.

History

after Robert Rozhdestvensky

History! / Picture me, a young man, so / naïve, so deeply
believing / and sincere / over your / absolutes, your palette
of trues. Your / precision of gradient
and angle, / indisputable as a math; / less
questionable / than cliché. / But boys
age, become / grown. Your wind / shades their skin /
and the seconds now / are demanding account
of the centuries. / I write / in the name
of the seconds…

History / has the fructose / beauty of dawn. / History
has the grand / grind of poverty,
structuring people anew / before / scuttling off
in the face of their / degradation. History, /
correct / and senseless. Recall, / now, how frequent
you're called / *appalling*, though / breathtaking, or /
noble though shocking, / shameful, /cruel.
How you depended / on passing / fashion, on ego
and conception: / on dumb façade. How you / shrank
from the dictators / who measured you by / their own
invented versts and the scrabble / of inches.
Proclaiming your / name, they / stupefied the peoples,
claimed / your protection, and made / worlds, /
lands. You have allowed yourself / to be
powdered, / history, again: rouged and / made up,
again, and redyed, / and again fitted
for a suit of new black. / You were / redrafted / to that
army / of / raucous cries / specialising
in switching / 'great men' / for people:

History! Whore. / *History!* Queen. / You are not
the dust, drying / in archives. History, /
clutch these whispering fingers, / open your
living heart / to the people. / Look, / how
sensibly / your founders, / your
managers and copers / are waking, / are

swallowing their / humble breakfast. / They are hurrying
to kiss their wives, / their goodbyes. The greenery /
of scent covers them, so / excitingly, the high / sun
beats in their eyes, / the horns / flourish their / noise,
and the imperturbable smoke / rises endlessly / from the chimneys; /
cries its tired praise against / the still sweep / of skies.
You will, / history, / you will be yet / the most exact
gauge and measure, / the sweet geometry
of pressure. You / will be. You must. It is so / longed-for.

Of Some Substance, Once

and for all there is no other thing
in which the soul or any soul-like thing consists:
clear as lipstick is lips. Or the free will
of one hand, moving for another: a vanity. A sun,
spun around the Earths we weave of ourselves.

I do not say this. I watch you watching the moon.
And any moment I will take my chest and I will kiss you.
For the first time. So to the materialist I say:
if you cannot ride two horses at once
you shouldn't be
                    in the circus.

Coming to Pass

after Hölderlin's fragment: 'Reif Sind, in Feuer getaucht, gekochet…'

I

The way fruit, arriving
at its moment of ripeness, is glazed with fire,
cooked and checked by the earth's close process. It's law,
after all, how all things come to pass,
temptress but unearthly. And as
the heavy stake of kindling, resting
on the shoulders, there is much to bear
in mind. But the trails
are evil. And everything
bridled will anyhow
wander off, like horses
into dusk; everything
shot through with this longing
to go beyond bounds. But so much
stands to be lost. And loyalty
a must; which rules out prophecy
or nostalgia. Let us surrender, be rocked –
cradling ourselves against the moment –
like a boat, lapped by the waves.

II

For a moment the project
will come perfectly to fruition,
each word glossed by its
plunge into the fire of the present, that flicker
from which everything is once again
made anew. It's almost gospel
the way things arrive, slip askew,
and depart: as a snake,
dreaming of the cloths of heaven, its mounds
of laundry, its drying lines. And as
the weighted intellect, kindle

to any moment's inspiration
or distraction, there is much to bear
in mind. And the previous versions
of the damn thing verge
on the diabolical. And everything
you think you've got bridled, every axiom
you've nailed, will wander off, like horses
into dusk, appearing
to dissolve into the dust of secondary
and tertiary meanings. And the constant
temptation to reach beyond what's
suitable, beyond bounds, into the dense red
of yourself, your vague
and useless gloss. And so much,
so much stands to be lost! And loyalty
a must: this raking up of foreign soil,
the spoiled quarantine of adherence
to original is no good. No good. All of which
rules out the possibility of prophecy,
or nostalgia. Let us rock between the two,
like a little skin-keeled coracle on a sea of confusion,
lapped by the various camberings
of serial and distinct waves, one
after the other, made up
of the exact same water.

Vahni Capildeo

The question 'Where are you from?' requires resistance. I work 'from' a place that would be pigeonholed if named but whose multiplicity liberated my imagination. Caribbean writers have a tradition of crafting words, rather than defining themselves by genre or occupation; there is no hard contradiction between poet, journalist, Carnival maker, festival programmer, Ministry worker, housewife, judge – only the tensions of everyday survival. Betrayal and connexion sing from the unfair trade and travel routes of the archipelago and its Americas; so even the lyric's context and time zone are expansive. Trinidad's languages, from the First Peoples, Africans, Indians, Chinese, Syrian/Lebanese, Europeans, make various music continually in my mind, bearing blissfully dissonant ways of understanding and making images about the world. Pronouns such as 'I', 'you' and 'we' are sites of love and struggle still in process, not items for theoretical play or attack. New technologies will be crucial in bringing kindred spirits and innovators into conversation across sea, space and local answerabilities.

from Inhuman Triumphs

(iii)
The Poet Transformed into a Heat Haze

& it was not a hot country; but occasionally
hot, though not by decree nor description; even a day
like this, where it rained fiercely on sheets of sun, jubilant
about heat, but denying hotness; not a hot country.
& it drove the insects in droves, it drove drivers off roads,
drove drivers into whatever grows on the sides of roads
& roads became what happened to be passing by, because
I melted them; & beggars died too shy to beg for drinks
because it's stupid to feel the heat, admit to feeling
the heat & to not liking it & not to liking it
but to feeling everything twice as thick, feeling at all;
the stream sucked it up, milled on wordless; the trees rebelled, O
love, voted with their roots, forgetting how to vote, vowing
their all to – as a leaf double, shape, shade, light – a stitch-up –

Pobrecillo Tam

Only I do not like the fashion of your garments. You will say
they are Persian attire, but let them be changed.
                                        – King Lear, III.vi.

        raise yr game said my friend lucky
        in love since going online
        to learn moves that lead from geek
        to playa. go to the big
        baldwin city; life's laid out like
        yr sister's tea set that time
        she spilled the milk & didn't
        cry for a real melting knife.
        chamoised my head & was going,
        radiant as a hermit's cave

in cappadocia; fled Him
& my other dogs & wall–
papered my sister's braced smile
in carious photographs.
well caramel you can cross,
pass, shoot for the stars, scrape sky
for a living but don't hang
yr washing from the window –
the old man doesn't like it;
& see that tree? it translates
spring will bring again bread stone
scorpion to hand; always
afternoon if once you stand
in His light. i prayed for lift-off
& became a little horse
shadowed by an always car;
i prayed for inside, needed
shadow like a crown on my head,
lived off foods composed of sub–
stitutions. Lady of sit–
uations, i pray for lift–
off, tailoring my head & bust
to rise above this city
of unkadare nature,
pushkin types, fatalistic
pedestrians who're at the start
of my game, who're my true loves,
if only their hearts were Gabriel,
& not being borgesed to death
staying off the drive-by streets,
mummified in the seven
sealed orifices firstnamed home.

Slaughterer

The tears curled from the cattle's eyes, their horns curled back, their
coats curled like frost-ferns on windshields or the hair on the heads
of Sikandar's soldiers. Two of my grandfather's sons, when he knew
he was dying, took him from his bed. They supported him out the
doorway so he could say goodbye to his favourite cattle. The cattle
wept. They knew him. They are not like cattle here. They live among
the household and on the hills, which are very green, and they eat good
food, the same food as the household, cut-up pieces of leftover chapatti.

You do not get stories like that in books. I am telling you because
you only have things to read. Whenever anybody tried to make me read
a book or anything, I would fall asleep; my head would just drop.

What is the use of reading books? What can you do after that but
get an office job? Do my friends who stayed at school earn as much as
me? They all have office jobs; could they do a job like mine? Could
they slaughter for seventy hours without getting tired or needing to
sleep?

It was hard at first. I used to dream the cattle. They would come
to me with big eyes, like mothers and sisters. After a few weeks, they
stopped coming to me in dreams. After about five years, I stopped
feeling tired: I do not need to sleep. We do three or four thousand a day
in Birmingham, only a thousand a night in Lancaster.

Tonight I am going to Lancaster. I will talk to you until Lancaster.
Where are you from? You are lying on me. No, where are your parents
from? Are you lying on me? I came here as a teenager, and at once they
tried making me read. How old are you? Why do you only have things
to read? I am sorry I am talking to you. You have brought things you
want to read. Beautiful reader, what is your name?

You can feel the quality of the meat in the animal when it is alive:
the way its skin fits on its flesh. You can feel the quality of life in the
meat. The cattle here are not good. They inject them. Their flesh is
ahhh.

Look, look how beautiful. I will show you pictures of the place.
Look, it is very green.

Fire & Darkness: And Also / No Join / Like

O Love, that fire and darkness should be mix'd,
Or to thy triumphs such strange torments fix'd!
                                   – John Donne, Elegy XIII

A northern street: the temperature of the ungovernable. The
proud hooded stride. The skill to add up stone: cold – outlasting. The
wealth of the land: stone. Kindness: the harsh kind. For each question,
a better question. For each better question, one answer. For each good
question – that'll do. Not fussed.

I walk the hollow walk: loving more than loved; moved, scarce
more than moving.

                                                          and also

In the south of this country, five times I have attended the
celebrations that they hold in the dark of the year. Many centuries
ago, there was a man whose name was Guy, or Guido. He practised a
different, competing version of the national religion. He tried to explode
an important government site. These buildings are still in use. You can
visit the place, which is on the river. Some of the children who ask for
money on British streets are simply trying to fund their construction of
effigies of this hate figure, whose burning on public and domestic pyres
on the so-called 'Bonfire Night' (5 November) has become a popular
ritual. Fireworks are let off; it is legal to purchase them for your own
festivities.

                                                          no join

A northern street, uphill. It branches, like – a Y, a peace sign,
water coursing round an outcrop; like – part of the net of a tree; like –
It branches in two. Upon the slope held between the branches stands a
sooty church, now in use as a nightclub. This pale and brisk morning
glances on the metal railings.
Who is he?
Nobody.
Who is he, between the fence and lamp post?
Nobody. A hat stuck on the railing, abandoned by a tidy drunk. A
feeble visual joke. Nobody's head, nobody's, supports a hat drooped at

that angle.

It is a guy. A Guy Fawkes guy. The students left him there: lad for the burning: unreal, it has to be unreal. Check out this guy.

I have to cross the road, so I do.

The ordinary-looking foot is wedged between the base of the fence and the lamp post. The left arm, bent at the elbow, has been tucked deep into the jacket pocket, toneless. It is not a bad face. The eye is the pity of it: tender lids tightened into a crescent, as happens with mortally wounded birds; infolding, no longer able to yield, a turning inwards of the ability to light up.

I put my hand into my pocket, for my phone.
It is not necessary.

Pale and brisk as this morning, the police car slides into my peripheral vision.

and also

A street in Trinidad: the soft, brown 'ground doves' have the same manners as the pedestrians. Unhurried, they traipse along in front of cars. Why did the ground dove cross the road? I don't know, but it's certainly taking its time.

The exception came plummeting out of the recessive sky, into the back yard's concrete rain gutter. Had a neighbourhood boy felled it inexpertly? Had the ecstatic efficiency of its heart thumped to a stop? It lay there, the softness, and would not, could not bestir itself.

The child strewed it with yellow and scarlet wild lantana flowers, thinking of burial, accustomed to cremation; feeling a sudden fear. The parents took it all away.

And when the dove was gone, another came plummeting the same way; the riddle repeated – to be moved, moving, and never to move. Love or some other force was identical in the equation.

no join

We brought few friends home who were not already part of at least a two-generation family circle. We brought few friends home. This time my brother had introduced a soft and brown and tallish young man in his early twenties, who weighed not much more than a hundred pounds. By historical pattern, not personal choice, in our secular Hindu household, this was the first Muslim friend our age.

Perhaps it has changed; but non-Indo-Caribbeans used not to be aware that 'Ali' and 'Mohammed' are not 'Indian' names. And in that unawareness they are linguistically wrong, but more profoundly right: for our ancestors brought over a shared Indian village culture, over a century before the creation of Pakistan in the Indus area made such a difference. And in that Trinidad remote from Trinidad's Trinidad, and nonetheless most mixed and Trinidadian, a lunatic reverberation was set up by the 1947 Partition – some third-generation immigrant families briefly fought according to the lines of what had not been a division. In lands far away, current events were indirectly regenerating or inventing this part of Trinidad's past also. By 1990, we knew that there must be some difference.

We sat on the nice imported sofa with the delicate novel unicorn visitant who looked just like us.

All over the island, every evening just before seven, telephone calls were wound down, fires turned low beneath pots, and families converged on the television set to listen to the news headlines: a link with the greater world. Nothing was expected to happen.

A square, reliable face showed up.

'The liberation of Kuwait has begun.'

The look of devastation and betrayal on our guest's face was like nothing I could have imagined seeing. An outline seemed to be sitting in his place, while the person who had occupied that outline crumbled.

Why? Televised missile fireworks were going off, white and purple. What had so upset him?

I tried to see with his eyes. Brownskinned people with strong features and children of adorable gravity were being killed from the air; and en masse they looked more like us than anyone else on television, local or international, in those days. My insides flipped. People who looked like they could be family were being killed from the air.

We are not evolved to cope with aerial threats. To witness the spectacle of bombing is to feel guilty and due to be wiped out; for all our gods inhabit the heavens, and to be safe our earliest kind might have taken to the trees, where only the gods could smite them. To be bombed is to be smitten by the wrath of a Deity not to be located and not in our image. To ascend into Heaven becomes profoundly and secretly inconceivable; for the borders of the heavens are guarded with fire.

Was this what our friend was seeing? The starring roles in war, in our young memories, hitherto had been for people who did not look like us. Or was he seeing war upon his religion?

From now on, anyway, in the world's play of representations of the living, we would look more like the killed. We would resemble – like it or not – anti-advertisements for flourishing societies; which is perhaps why people on the street in the south of England have told me that they have no money, or have offered me money, when I have said nothing or when I was about to ask for directions and certainly have not had a guy to burn.

Our soft brown young man sat, and sat, until he could get himself home.

no join

no join

no join

and also

like

like

like

from Louise Bourgeois: Insomnia Drawings

Edinburgh, Fruitmarket Gallery, 2013

for Rod Mengham

She Courted Sleep by Drawing Sheep, Then One Was Drawn to Her

friend sheep, if i stretched wide enough
i could give birth to a child like you:
a round-eyed barrier against normality,
a rare breed indeed, not a marie antoinette pet.
legendary plus que prehistoric.
a sheep like you at my knees
and pre-ruined trade routes at my feet,
and we would be in Sumeria.

dans la nuit it was lost, a closet heterosexual;
my children's successful sleep rendering me antimaternal
as if my body had not gaped, was a gap, was immaterial.
so I placed my hands between my legs, found fleece,
began to pull, till wonderstruck i ushered you
into my studio, away from the world, from the waking world.

peaceable and only slightly sinister
since languageless and eager in your bleating
about the silence brushing up against us from all sides,
my darling newborn ancient beast,
unboxed and not for sacrifice.

i count on you. take us away.
cross another and another stile.
nibble your way through the hedge of mist
springing from the Hudson,
through the thorns of light thrown up
by the Atlantic; voyage safely, amicable sheep,
into France; no questions asked.

i would flatten with you into tapestry,
my hair and yours washed by handfuls in the river,
vu que, in profound night and these circonstances,
it is déjà as if insomnia hangs us, already
hooked to a wall.

Simple Complex Shapes

Rain is falling gently on a sloping roof.
How am I to stay awake?

Leopardcats petition for their morning meats,
piteous, round-mouthed.

Look for them till you no longer
look at them. Bright sky.

They could not make a home with you
nor wait at home for you;

always they go home in you,
every happy solitude.

Stalker

for K.M. Grant

He waits. Without knowing me,
he waits. The tips of branches,
edible and winey, bring
spring by suggestion to him
who in autumn dawn, eager,

with wet knees, disregards me,
being drawn by me. He waits
and in me he waits. I branch,
the form is branching, it bounds
like sight from dark to bright, back
again. The form is from me:
it is him, poem, stag, first sight
and most known. In him I wait:
(when he falls) needs must (hot heap),
nothing left over (treelike
no longer) nor forlorn: we're
totalled.

Mercy and Estrangement

His heart hurtling towards me
I not caring to catch it
it turns into a bird, turns:
a scavenger bird lightfoot
alights on foam, contests white
as silver tilts white, silver
as refuse seams silver, gawks,
jinks, is radiated by charts
charted inly: magnetic,
unhoming because transformed.
A rill and jitter brought me
– birdform, my heart – to the park
where state translators, laid off,
sat sad for their hospitals,
prisons and schools. Laws whistled
infixes between trained ears.
And at our conference,
so many equivalents
for *gracias* and *Verfremdung*,
easy change amongst false friends.

The Prolongation of the Spine and the Stretched Neck Approximate the French Philosopher Only to his Own, and Airy, Beast

after Georges Bataille, 'La Bouche'

★

The mouth is planetary, circled by systematic tides. The molten core, the tongue-root; the microbial cities; the sirocco and austerities of breath.

★

The mouth is geographical to the extent that the body is terrain. The tiny life of flaking skin and self-mating thighs may exist and teem without language; the python inhabiting the buccal cavity may remain uninterpretable, too big to be perceived, by the atheistic dermal crowd.

★

The mouth is engineered by gender. In grief and anger, my sister's mouth will twist into a trap, it will not drop to let out the paroxysmal bellow which would be permitted her in childbirth; however and alas, her mouth seals itself, even her lips turn in as her eyes widen and the sinews in her neck become unmusically, why not furiously, strung.

★

The mouth is an anemone. See, in the dark wood it flowered and, sensing something, your hair raised up; but the social occasion smoked over your possible paths into the dark wood that flowered with promise and that tussored over the sleeping area of snakes.

★

The mouth is half of a knot. With my lips I tie you; our bodies are boat and floating jetty, our cinched animality no doubt locatable by the anxious Frenchman, who is rendered anxious because we have unnerved the chapterhouse of his skull and outside his studious window, oh so

suddenly, cry after cry unnerves the night, as we prolong the ground
as sea beneath his feet, as we slip (mouths knotted) out from the erotic
vessels of ourselves, careless of the power to hurt or to do none.

Lesley Saunders

These poems exemplify two preoccupations in my writing – trying to create credible connections between then and now, there and here, other and self; and trying to find the right tone. I studied Latin and Greek at university decades ago and the allure of those languages and their worlds is as strong as ever. The poets I admire, past or present, refuse to be limited to or by the ego's ailments: there's no shortage of 'I's in their work, but the first person is not, or not to be taken as, autobiographical. Or that's not where their poetic energy lies – the aches and pains are distilled, alchemised, so that it's the reader who ends up feeling more fully herself. That's what I'm after, to get myself out of the way of the poem. I think that's why collaborations, residencies, researched projects, even ekphrastic sequences (such as the Remedios Varo poems), play such an important role for me: there's a reality to be reckoned with, a resistance that the poetry has to negotiate, weigh itself against, try to be equal to. And that's a question of tone as much as anything else – such an elusive thing to get right...

Indigo

There's a colour at the back of things
    sombre and shining: ceremonial sky, seas

of ripening wheat, a dolphin reconnoitred
    through spume. The darkening surface of time

as it passes. The northerly sea-lanes,
    sea-glass carved into currencies,

opportunity like a sail on the horizon.
    The irises in a blond stranger's gaze,

his shoals of soft stinking cloth,
    a new kind of blue that's been wrung

out of green, vegetal not heavenly.
    A dyer's fingernails indelibly stained

the ultramarine of the veins on her hands.
    The flung-out *ikats*. The distances.

Landfall

> *Charaxus has arrived!*
> *His ship was full!*
>   – Sappho, the Brothers poem,
>   trans. Christopher Pelling

One can imagine a brother. I played alone
in a back garden far from the sea among
my father's roses; jet trails feathered
    the endless summer sky,

    daylight sailed the coastline of my room.
    I prayed at night though not for him,
    out there in the deep of a universe
        whose horizons swerved

far beyond the reach or sway of any mercy
I could think of. After roses, the blue
and gold of asters, cold stars to navigate
     the year's vast tides by.

There's a name for what I feel, though
I don't know it yet, my Greek still falters
over words for unharvested, heart-heavy.
     Barythymia: all at sea.

Olfactory

Shall you have no pity for me?
                – Philoktetes

As he basked in that Aegean island noon,
the ocean brochure-azure, asphodels glossy
and stiff as symbols, he didn't need to pluck
at his shirt, stick his nose in his pits to know
it was him: source of volatile organic compounds,
mobile oil-factory of sun-rotted whale,
first in the telegenic line of embarrassing bodies.
The leaflets in Greek that dropped on the shingle

were telling him to pack his kit, make ready for Troy
after all. The sense of smell fatigues quickly,
he hopes, though he knows from his *temps perdu*
how shocking the odour of bodies can be,
Herakles' sweat on his flesh, the salt-fish
stink of his sex, still washing over him in waves
of longing, disgust. He tries to classify its notes:
pungent, musky, camphoraceous, *kai ta loipa*

– and what about the menthol-madeleine moment
of shared cigarette, silk-cut on linked fingers,
sweet reek of love? His foot aches inexpressibly,

clostridium perfringens eating his gristle, tendons,
his pedestrian bones, reworking them as gangrene, stench.
It was the snake, a poisoned arrow, the consequence
of chronic smoking, it was vengeance or penance,
it was quitting or failure to quit, it was a curse

or a cure in itself. It was him.

Army Musician

Endless files of them, and caissons, commissary wagon trains, ambulances,
herds of cattle. Drummer boys beating the pace with each company…
                                    – E.L. Doctorow, *The March*

Enveloped in wet turf
all these bloodless years
like a vellum psalter
or ancestral soul,
deaf to muffled voices
of rescuers overhead,
a six-inch frame drum

surfaces through a sky
of mud, moon-faced,
its veiled questions
how long from, how far since
and whether it was morning
or afternoon when the tune
in his head deserted him

like a flight of quail
or shooting stars; whether
he could then or afterwards
in the march-past of silences,
magnificent, tobacco-laden,
in the spent blue of evening,
all fifes and bugles gone,

have cut a makeshift whistle
from a horsetail-reed
or fathomed the actions
of small heroic birds wheeling
and manoeuvring
in the pools of air
a hair's-breadth above him

Impasse

Elephants are easily terrified, the brightness
bouncing off the ice crystals burns their eyes.
Rome is still a week away down breakneck scarps

and frozen roads; half the corps are sick,
snow-blind and heart-sick. The light here is full
of damage, white, white, you must blacken

the skin beneath your eyes with charcoal lest
the glare, like a hawk who drives death into
a prey's brain with her middle claw, transfix you.

Some days we offer no resistance to the light,
we are stranded above the snowline, above
the drop, and our tears are unstoppable.

Census

for the National Statistician

My dreams are still at it, the royals and rough sleepers
and the secret many sitting at my table spilling coffee

on the questionnaire, inserting the small statistical errors
that conceal names and places, microdata of selves

tiptoeing in from Domesday. Counting only the people,
how many visitors are staying overnight! And have we

enough sheets for them all? Others are street-partying
through the wee grey hours, and for person 5 there is a tick

next to son or daughter. Remember to include the babies.
There is so much responsibility. (Oh but is there time

to lift your eyes from the screen, peer at the sloe blossom
pale as rice, as iced water, like a blur in the trees?) The house

I grew up in looks ordinary now but the questions read aloud
fall like mystic verse on the ear. So much responsibility,

while we go on living parted from. Do not count
anything you do barefoot as part of your paid employment,

there is a spring-like randomness in the universe's heart.
If this is not the life you meant to live, please ask

for help. We belong to the beloved. How would you
describe. How well can you speak. How long can you stay.

Gaudete

Season of candlelight
and ice-fairs, a moon

no more than a nail-paring,
as lead-white and radiant

as a dancer starving
for the pharma of touch,

her bird-bones an x-ray
of separation. Reach up

and hold her fingertip.
Its weight will amaze you.

Particulare Care

pray Let particulare care be taken off this child, As it will be call'd for Again
        — note left with Florella Burney at the Foundling Hospital

When I dream about the children, my boy my girl,
I dream them small-boned and wordless, as if again
I've turned my back, forgotten to come home

to feed them and need to find my way back to grace
beyond forgiving. Their dream-selves are always just-born
with their adult faces on, full of a sweet anxious daylight

I can barely look at, standing here on the edge
of deep water. I do not deserve them, these foundlings,
whom I will call out for again and again in the orphanage of night.

Personajes: Poems after Remedios Varo

1. Orinoco

Exploración de las fuentes del río Orinoco (oil on canvas, 1959)

Where does the self come from, with its soft hoods
and closed buttonholes?
Of what slubs and gabardines is it made?
Whose are its afternoons, those up-rivers paddled
by anxiety and boredom in the same measure,
whose little winged ship
in a forest of cut-out wishes?

Some of my selves, sombre and intrepid,
feel neither hunger nor thirst;
I do not know their names. They have gone on
without me.

Some of them are embroidered bowls
meekly appearing on every ledge of my palace
like cupped hands.
What can they catch but the serene news
of someone else's rescue,
seeps of light floating downstream
to where I fret with shame and envy?

Others wear their Schiaparelli next to the skin
– shoe-hat or lobster-dress, crocodillo,
veils and tears.
They canter on high-heeled pilgrimages
through the island's flooded woods
tuning in to documentaries on their boat-shaped radios.
It seems unlikely the source will find them.

The poles melt. The gazetteer is in the pocket I cannot reach.

2. Ascension

Ascensión al monte análogo (oil on triplay, 1960)

I wake on a small plank of early morning,
the night hours of unsupported self-study
abandoned for the wistful disciplines
of list-making, of listening to messages hidden
in my telephone – I'm infatuated with gadgetry,
how the newly sprung breeze fans my pinafore,
how my wristwatch escapes into a ship's quadrant.

The volcano behind me is full of digital spaces
like the empty-hearted bungalows
of an advanced society; its brook-waters
are everything to me. All day I surf the borders
of unrequited memory, navigating by fingertip.
This is not the end of the world, even if I buried
a box of lockets in the ash with their faces on.

If you would climb higher,
pay no account to public opinion. Don't
pick the flowers.
These two truths: it is already too late.
Be kind.

3. Laboratory

Creación de las aves (oil on Masonite, 1957)

Formula: I have my owl-mask on and the windows
that cannot be closed, I have made a miniature Stradivarius
to use as stethoscope; I have stoked the sensorium.

Modus operandi: a stylus, held in the painting hand,
is connected by the violin to the heart, you may feel
a quiet vibration in your chest-bones. The other hand

holds a magnifier. In separate pipettes, blood, egg, sky,
the primary birdsongs (this is not rocket science),
hatch their cantatas. I put on feather leggings,

sprinkle food. Outcome: a still-life of goldcrests
galvanised by rays of Pythagorean light, ensouled.
Try to attain a state of not-thinking; continue playing.

4. Minotaur

El minotauro (oil on Masonite, 1959)

Canto hondo. Bedtime stories.
There was a bull, his flanks white
as apple blossom, eyes blacker
than blood. Bull-I was down

on my snowy knees eating grass,
whisking flies. I was medicine.
Now all that's left of the lily ponds
and frescoed palace are its lino-tiles

and blank walls, the dust of koi-bones
in unswept corners. Or is it history
you want, a keyhole into the future?
At any moment the crescent moons

on my head will mutate into organs
of light, a hydraulics of heifer-milk
and Indian pearls; the squirm
in my right hand is an iron key

in a tight space, this unblinking gaze
is my poker face worn with a smile.
Covering your king with my queen
I sigh: Today of all days, the day

I began to smell like a woman,
the day I started washing the red
out of my clothes, I knew this was
my labyrinth, all its echoes

and strangers. As I tap-dance
on the tips of my mary-jane hooves,
you can see the placebo effect
is real, my costume period-perfect.

5. Personage

Personaje (oil on Masonite, 1958)

Nothing is what it seems, it takes
the entire span of the human voice
to improvise a space in the ruins
where the sense of weightlessness
can materialise, a pile of clothing
appear at the foot of a tree
like an undreamt dream. The room

grows yellower with dusk, its woods
point to underground water sources,
the still-sleeping *primum frigidum*,
or sometimes one of those silent dolls
a child describes her world with
behind closed doors. I was tearing up
bits of paper in the hope of finding

a way back, all I wanted was to live
without trash and the casual
discourtesies of the rich. The music
was distant, lunar, but these are not
the merciful things I set out to say.
I was leaning too far out of the window,
turning to absolute zero as I fell.

André Naffis-Sahely

These poems are episodes either from history or from the story of my life: episodes rescued, as Robert Lowell once put it, from 'amnesia, ignorance and education'. The business of living is too concerned with the pursuit of joy, thus distracting us from appreciating the magnitude of the moment as it occurs. Poetry rectifies that: it is the archaeology of memories; it is treasuring, by way of digging and recording.

Disposable Cities

They begin as rumours, snippets of exaggerated talk, too fabulous to believe, but too alluring to forget. *Something* has been found: gold, silver, rubber, uranium, coltan or oil. Before long, the promise of immeasurable wealth drowns all incredulity: they become barely visible blips on the horizon of prospects. The engineers in their hard hats and linens are the first on the ground, and with them come derricks, drills, platforms and dry docks. Pipelines sink their tentacles into every lucrative crevice marked on the map. The maps are kept secret.

A handful of shacks are erected to provide a few basic services. Soon enough, the handful swells into a hamlet, then a village, and finally a city. They are the perfect sort of settlement for the modern world: everything is shipped in and easily assembled. The cities have a primary and overriding purpose: to extract, process, and distribute. Just as a motorised pump draws water out of a well, they start inhaling people from all over the world, one desperado at a time.

At first, these new arrivals find their new 'homes' unsettling. They find it difficult to adjust to their weird climates and are frazzled by the confusion of languages. No one is under any illusions: they are ephemeral guests, non-citizens; belonging is a dream best forgotten or deferred. Most have come empty-handed, having traded their old lives for grubstakes. Lots of money sloshes around, but most of it is spent just staying alive, and when it runs out, people watch their lives fall apart. Everyone lives in a heightened state of awareness: one false move and they're gone. The poorer they are, the more modest their gambles, which more often than not make them poorer. 'Beggars don't build homelands', they tell themselves, fantasising about the day when they might return home and become someone.

Meanwhile, the myth travels to the four corners of the planet. More than cities, these El Dorados are a state of mind: places where people come to reinvent themselves and live out their most eccentric fantasies. All conurbations live out their lot and die, but these disposable cities are special: mushrooms of greed that can burst out of nowhere. Greenland, the Amazon, the Yukon, the Empty Quarter; areas of the world usually thought uninhabitable.

However, these cities' fame is fleeting. Once bled dry, their roads go raw with potholes, chickens roam loose in the opera houses, power-lines sag, and then rot seeps in and tars all in sight. Only those unlucky enough not to make it stay in town for the decline. One day, the wind howls and the last tent comes undone. The lie has moved on to the next disposable city. When I was a child, my mother used to tell me that lies had short legs, and thus could not get very far. Somebody lied to her.

Jumeirah Janes

A hill-station breeze blows through the café:
the ladies are dressed for high tea and the waiters
polish the windows that keep the hot sand at bay.

Life here has left a bitter film on their lips,
which they purse whenever one of them mentions
how her children have gone home and her husband

works six-day weeks even during the summer;
as if that weren't enough, the servants are lazy...
Then there are the locals, who are ignorant, venal,

tasteless and, even worse, lucky. The ladies
are lonely, they want to go back to the You-Kay.
'But then,' one says, 'we're so comfortable here',

at which point the conspiracy dies and like
moody nuns, the ladies nod in acknowledgement,
while their talk reverts back to the weather.

Abu Dhabi

Mina Zayed

It's early afternoon and the market looks like a used-car lot.
I watch men conduct business from the back of their trucks:
the epitome of the travelling salesman… There's not much

on sale today: spices, pots, bags of nuts, ceramic ashtrays –
a few customers stroll by, but it's too muggy to haggle.
The sleepiness of the place is broken only by the stinging,

oddly invigorating smell of diesel in the air. The port
is a short distance away, and the ships on the horizon
are like the humps on the great caravan of steel as it winds

its way from the West to the Rest. At the port, people talk
only of *will* and *shall*, as if the future had already happened.
A whole country is being built from scratch: there are cargo

containers as far as the eye can see. Meanwhile, the market
grows even more deserted, as if it were either the ragged
rear-guard of the past, or an inscrutable prototype of the future.

Abu Dhabi

A Summer Visit

for my mother

Our family has become a government-in-exile;
visiting you is like paying my respects
to a kindly downhearted minister who
is equally fearful of past, present and future.

Two small rooms to eat and sleep in; only
the essentials escaped being boxed up
while awaiting their destination. Still they wait.
This is home for now – a little town

outside Florence where the streets are lifeless
and the old stick their necks out of windows
like turtles keeping an eye out for vultures.
When apart, we speak only a little:

a pair of talking heads in a penumbra.
I look at you: a housewife without a house,
without a husband too. Pondering it all,
I chew anti-acids with a sovereign indifference…

Your younger son, your adjutant, or aide-de-camp,
shuts himself in his room all day and shoots aliens,
Nazis or terrorists on his console, almost
as if training for a war to reconquer our lives.

Florence

The Carpet that Wouldn't Fly

for my brother

You sport the sickly ecstasy of the exiles
that people your mother's favourite novels:
quiet, pale-faced, consumptive dreamers.
Your feet, once accustomed to soft sand,
fall heavier now. You lament the peculiar

European fetish for marble, its coldness.
Sometimes at night, in between cigarettes,
you pace the balcony and clap your hands,
as if expecting the cheap rug beneath you,
to flout reason and fly you back to the past.

Florence

A Kind of Love

We loved luxury and ate like pigs,
but our room, unborn as yet,
was bare; it was a new building,
and when we moved in, the landlord

looked us over and said: 'No noise
after eleven please'. Obediently,
for the most part, we adhered,
and kept the ancient record player

(among the only things of mine
to survive the neglect and the moths)
at its lowest; although money
was scarce, vinyl records were cheap

and we took advantage.
Halfway through the tenancy,
I got your name mixed up with
another woman's and, quite rightly,

without a word, you took your leave;
taking very little except the needle
you knew full well was irreplaceable,
unlike our short-lived kind of love.

Leicester

The Translator

for Michael Hofmann

Unshaven and barefoot, as if on a pilgrimage.
His house is blue: the walls, the carpet, the cups;
the kind of blue you see in sad monasteries,

the paint veined and peeling, with brittle bits of gold
hanging on in the rims. Like Gottfried Benn –
a spiritual father figure – he likes to stay home

where the coffee is better and there is no small-talk.
He seems scattered, has lost a book somewhere:
a translation. All his life he has hidden a language,

now he eats, breathes and interprets it. Later,
our awkwardness spilled over Hampstead Heath,
where we walked, mostly in silence. We had soup

and beer around the corner, then took a short-cut
to the bus stop, and he was gone; brought by the wind,
taken back by it: the soft-spoken wunderkind of despair.

London

Postcard from the Cape

for Declan, Parisa and Rachael

Few feet
tread the tired timber floors
of the old Observatory now, a couple
of tourists perhaps, or the odd
data analyst skulking in slippers
down the dark musty corridors.
The security guard is reading *The Pleasure Tube*,
'an exhilarating conspiracy aboard a sexy starship'.

There's no
star-gazing tonight and the clouds
stalk the yellow moon like hungry hyenas.
In 1820, when the Cape had that wet
smell of fever about it, Fearon Fallows
decided his work would devour his life,
and six years after his wife and children had died,
he'd installed his telescope atop Slangkop,

or 'snake hill',
as the Dutch colonists called it.
It's getting late, and the runaways
from the Valkenberg have grown hungry.
Little to eat today, just like yesterday too...
A few streets away, the Malay muezzin
clears his throat for the prayer call at the mosque
down in Salt River, past invisible lines

no whites
dare to cross. It's safer indoors,
inside panic mansions with Alsatians
and ARMED RESPONSE signs. David Shook
is in town – one night only! – on his way
to the lush land of Burundi, where the districts
are carved into mountains and the mayors
are 'king of the hill'. He tips an espresso

into a tall Coke,
'Haitian coffee', he says and we discuss
how travel often hardens the heart, and inures it
to shock, pity and pain… When dawn breaks,
I go into the garden and watch Devil's Peak
glow like a live coal. My myopia grows worse,
all I see is a blaze, but who needs high-definition?
If I close my eyes, the whole world feels like home.

Cape Town

Apparition

I was fooling myself I wasn't a tourist,
but shrewd, cunning and worldly;
a local, or at least, a dignified semi-local,
but out from a cavernous darkness

in the space between two crumbling houses
too narrow for a thigh, let alone two,
slipped a boy no older than twelve,
or was it ten perhaps? I'll never know…

His hand clamped my wrist. He was
too strong for a boy and his sharp cheeks
quasi-shadowed by stubble. It was clear
his childhood ended the day he could walk

and that he'd die the second he couldn't.
Gently, but firmly, as though herding
some lost sheep back to the fold, he
took me home, then asked for a most

modest sum for his efforts. I paid him.
He shook my hand. He had a mother
and four sisters waiting for him, but 'no men',
he said, pointing to three giggling chaps

smoking hash on the corner. 'Men,' he said,
pointing his index to the sky, as though
invoking some higher, infallible authority,
'men must work hard, or stay little forever.'

Fez

Mounting Mileage

I have just arrived in Kolkata after a thirty-six-hour train journey from
Chennai: a distance of fifteen hundred kilometres, which according to
my ticket has cost me a rupee per kilometre. I pull out a couple of these
coins from my pocket: they're incredibly slim, flimsy almost, like the
tinsel-wrapped chocolate doubloons I used to get given at Christmas.
Back then, I fantasised I could use them to fund a lavish lifestyle on
some tropical island. It wasn't long, however, until I learned that travel
required real money; and lots of it. Over time, I have worn countries
like shirts or shoes, and shed bits of myself in each. Fragments I'll never
recover. I'm still young, but it already appears obvious that the places I
visit and come to love will die before my very eyes, replaced by different
versions that soon someone younger will come to know and appreciate.
This frenetic sort of travelling may simply be my way of 'appeasing
the fear of the fugitive', as a German philosopher once put it, but my
mounting mileage has only increased my inclination to move; not
merely to scatter my dust, but because I know that whatever the soul is,
travel feeds it. And that the soul is not so trivial or small a thing, that I
should stifle it to take care of my stomach.

Nyla Matuk

I write these poems as reactions to our increasingly disembodied experiences, which have largely replaced embodied experiences in built environments – a consequence of long hours spent communicating via computers. It is a paradox, but communicating with each other in this way is characterised by the loss of a particular kind of self-estrangement, a route to access a sort of hunger, or appetitive experience of the world. The psychoanalytical writer Adam Phillips' idea that 'you can only recover your appetite, and appetites, if you can allow yourself to be unknown to yourself' seems important to me because it underscores the sense of wonder about the self that is missing when we spend so much time identified to others via technology by name, handle, avatar, or other flattened, outward markers. I contemplated the compelling idea of 'appetite' in these poems under other guises as well: for instance the figure of the haunted stranger in 'Appetites', or the sense of the uncanny in 'Meditation After Seeing *Hannah Arendt*'. The operationalisation of hermeneutical thought, in 'Aquatic Hermeneutics', is a related inquiry, an exploration of what we might exegetically know of what is ultimately strange: the sea; and the surrealist exploration of what is sublime in 'Grandeur' hints at what I might label the 'appetitive unknowable'.

Meditation After Seeing *Hannah Arendt*

I go see Barbara Sukowa as Hannah Arendt in Margarethe von Trotta's
Hannah Arendt. The audience is made to understand how, following orders,
Eichmann was simply himself; how Arendt substantiated *banality of evil.*

I leave the theatre. I go straight home and study Wordsworth's
"Ode: Intimations of Immortality from Recollections of Early Childhood."
I consider all the nature in it, and I try to understand the power of the
inevitable.

They say power lies in arbitrariness. At any time, the consequences
of disobedience may become apparent. They say freedom is being free
of domination. We are free if the State does not interfere, arbitrarily or
otherwise.

On Monday, in my office building, I look out
the seventh floor window down on a copse of trees
swaying in the May wind. Later, I see trees in front of houses

on the street, their green jewels dancing. Those leaves
in the sunshine remind me of a kind of ending, but not death. Only
the idea of it, arbitrarily and ordinarily rushing through us, without
interference.

Aquatic Hermeneutics

Sea monsters inside sea shells.
See, inside each shell, a sea monster.
Hear the peals of sea monsters like bells.

Boys riding their friendly dolphins.
Dolphins, with their waving fins.
Wave to the boys, dolphins, wave to the bluefins.

She got violet candy from her suitors.
Grandmother's rakish hucksters.
Sailors with candy saw her hooters.

A Coco de Mer nut washed ashore,
like buttocks splayed on the beach.
Godzilla's nuts shrunk by a leech.

A giant tuna circles the Boston Aquarium.
Others give the dame a wide berth.
Her body is fat and shiny, a turquoise diamond;
As we know, a dame needs diamonds.

Boarded a P&O ferryboat at Portsmouth
with my cig-holder smoking aunt Belle.
All night I bobbed in that berth heading south.
Melting in my pockets, salted caramel.

A kimono folds like the funereal gift of sushi;
a fish swims through the breeze in the anemone.
Future garnishes for the fattiest of fillets but
its body is still young, svelte as the manta ray.

Ocean amplified by the sound of hartshorn;
around the Horn of Africa, antlers curled.
The hunter's bugle sharper than a French horn.
Waves in the ocean whirled and hurled.

Hear the peals of sea monsters like bells.
See, inside each shell, a sea monster.
Sea monsters inside sea shells.

A Current

Here I come in my suit of insignificance,
hewn to importance. How revolutionary,

these days, for everyone to stop *identifying*
with the art, and to start treating it as just that—art.

A roar and a mandarin self. Found in this shell's
swirl, I'm content to say I wear the *vita brevis* well.

Walk miles through terra cotta death masks;
the diaphanous transmogrifications crossed

over lifetimes are still missing. So it goes for that old
shipping line, the spectacle of the heart. Or the tidal tedium

of thought without feeling. Freud had his beautifully wrought
staircase in his inner vestibule, a peculiar Viennese canard.

It's wrongly assumed that understanding rests at a lyric angle,
that love can undo bad misunderstandings in one afternoon.

I believe someone will look at me one day,
his eyes empty of everything but tenderness.

I watch winter from the window, every few
years studying the storms, who speak

to each other. Memory is only looking down
into the fragile stairwell of a nautilus.

Appetites

You wake hearing the girl next door come in at two a.m.
　　　　In the event that it is a ghost, it's telling you
that you shouldn't be wasting time in bed
　　　　　　worrying.
　　　　　　You should be sleeping, or doing
　　　　　　anything else.
　　　You haven't yet seen the faun, the red fox,
　　　　　　or the rabbit.

　　　The statue of a woman in the lily-padded lake is waist-deep,
　　　a mimicry of Diana's animal life, suspicious of sleep.

With her in mind, you're troubled even thinking of things
　　　　that don't frighten you.

But this, too, is a waste of time and talent.

There is good slumber
to be sought in the rush of ruminations outside yourself:
　　　in listlessness of reeds on the dead embankment,
　　　　　in languor of bee by a late marigold
　　　　　　　or duck feathers gathering in a corner of falling water.

A drowse of duck down keeps a person warm.

You wake up and try to pick up the thread.

You realize you haven't organized your life.

You've forgotten yourself entirely,

　　　so happy to find

　　　you have an appetite.

Grandeur

*Is this gorgeous exterior a mere false and clumsy pageant, which if laid open will be found
to conceal nothing but emptiness? For if so, a noble mind will scorn instead of admiring it.*
                              — Longinus, *On the Sublime* (trans. H.L. Havell)

An incognito species of gold.
Rue the day, *soupe du jour*.

Creep of surf, roll of clouds in a
doom of fluff, save only for a gathering
funnel of sunlight—
Eggshell closed the widening
gyre of that life.

I tried Zen once but I disliked
bowing and robes.
Bow to the Master!
And bow again.
And bow again.
Eggshell, a condition so servile, so fragile;
the colour itself a
bourgeois notion masquerading
as real life.

Just as Anacreon, poet of the sensual, mastered hedonism's populism,
so Sappho's love ode, with sublimity of purpose and an eye
on the dark nightingale, retreated from base flash.

Love had not evaporated; rather, eggshell was never its best suit.
And who is that coconut always walking beside you?
Full of blustery indignation, these eggshell symbols.
Mad Marge, in a barge, rowing to Hell and back.
Summer's wild skillet? Hell. And so, work with it!

They put artistic recognition in a jar. Called it Fluff™,
took advantage of the humble Marshmallow.
Why?
Because it resembles clouds, and sleep, from afar, and
a spy they called Eggshell.

The powdered wig of past French regimes.
Tiaras of emerald and ruby.
I told you: *it's not just for house-painting enthusiasts any more.*
I'm calling Fluff™'s bluff though.

I loved the summer haze coming
off the lake, too. Home again, and
gazing down into the fireplace's orange horror.
Orange. Horror. Colour. Terror. Motor. *L'horloge manqué.*
Late again. The clocks wound down, deflated.
Finality or *finale*? There is weight in such a choice.
Above us, scudding clouds project their mannerist cinema
while we twinkle below. They marble and recombine.
The funerary animal wears a shroud—a jackal in a sarong.
You apparatchik clouds, listen.

Mimes

I open the door to find a storm.
Twenty rooks busy at worms
abandon the green hillside and disappear

in the branches. Even animals who know
their place in the system will hide.
Leaving the trees, they reach

dissonant suspense. It's a long overture.
With no help from their elders,
they beat their wings and squawk.

Most animals and clouds choose to live
in a thunderstorm with their familiars.
No story I could tell you about

---

them would do justice.
Still, it's in our nature to ask them
to repeat their gestures. Birds, clouds,

and other vulnerables
flutter in the wordless present.
Any moment now, they'll break

character. They teach me how
to behave. I have no double.
They don't say a thing.

Happenings on the Cover of the *New Yorker*

after James Schuyler

Huddles of French threes hunch over their tables
at Bemelmann's Bar in a cinematic perfumery,
unaware their champagne—*champers*, I mean—
fête champêtre, drew the ire of an American promised
a good table, by the *maître d'*, the table he gets Thursdays.

An Ivy Leaguer with a BlackBerry sits alone
in a carpet-bag-lined alcove, had come in from Southampton
that morning more manned than ever in Ralph Lauren.
His style is cordial and matches the service. He orders

a Hemingway daiquiri, listens in to a docent sweeping poetic
on Edward Hopper's "New York Movie." *I believe Hopper
had alienated majesty.* A notion like that arrives like a spring-pink
blush—floating, enlightened—a moveable new idea. *"There's the*

loud alarm of a new orange idea," someone said. Then the French think
of a droll irony, which they love to do, and this time it's a big picnic and
big snowflakes outside on Madison Avenue, and that Woody Allen
was here. The beveled windows at Bemelmann's bedeviled

the chickadee girl, the one with a fat yarn ribbon in her hair
and a lipstick drawing fantasy for the powder-room mirror. The American
approaches the huddle and says, *Are you French? You must be French
because you're very rude!* And the Hieronymous Bosch brownies

Bemelmans doodled on the walls all shook in their boots, hearing
such frank talk. The second Mrs de Winter was a small part of the

pantomime.

We knew it was winter. The Winter, de Winter—they are one, but they're
not the same. O what a troubled little republic.

Claudine Toutoungi

Writing a poem for me is chaotic; it happens in fits and starts, sometimes on the hoof, sometimes not. It might be provoked by rage, injustice, a new love or an old wound, but I'm often unsure of the driving force until quite late on and forcing the question usually ends in everything backfiring. I like Gloucester's line in *King Lear*, 'I see it feelingly'. It seems to validate the art of stumbling towards sense, relying on whatever instincts can be mustered and (in the case of writing a poem) the energy of the words themselves. The jumping-off point for 'Midtown Analysis', for instance, was something concrete, the looming edifices of Manhattan, but by the time I'd stirred the soup of images the city gave me – snippets from menus, details from a guided tour of a skyscraper – the poem had evolved into a strange, psychic drama all of its own.

Winter Wolf

I was in a
  hypnagogic state
    when he arrived/

I couldn't move.

I registered sound hazily as
    Father Christmas moving round the
        furniture/ televisual rumbles

from the Next Door Fan of Japanese
    cartoons/ the scud of branches
        unhinged by the storm.

No pawing at the door
    could be for *us,*
      not *this* night.

I was lulled –

so when I found the tree up-
    turned and scalped of needles, angels
      dismembered, presents gone,
        the carpet

studded with glass,

    I felt almost serene to see what I
      had missed/ the long un-
        wished for caller

come at last.

Without Moorings

Yesterday when you were upset, I
wanted to tell you – things get
rubbed out all the time,

faces, thoughts, lines of
communication. Take this empty space,
around which the artist has sketched

the beige sizzle of hot sand, the cry of an out–
of-sight gull, the breath of a sleeping child
sighing behind drawn-down blinds.

All the people in it have left, or died or
are in hiding and even the unmanned boats go nowhere,
save for one without moorings

nosing towards freedom
on a fishless sea.

Bolter

I can see why you would.
You're equine enough for starters. Shall we say jerky?
A fine, thoroughbred sort of jerk, twitchy as hell, with a long trail
                                          of turf in your wake.

You look down on me from your high place, Emperor of Horses,
ears cocked for thunder and your eyes,
your eyes are two thirds lid.

They do and do not shut me out.
Their single line of light,
my stern reminder

– *Don't pat this one. Don't feed him sugar.*

Cats Breakfasting

after John Craxton's painting Cretan Cats

The meat of the fish is long gone.
Its smiling bones intersect with the back of a chair,
laid out pat, one more rung in a stack
and the velvety cats can't leave it alone.

There's no word for this in the language of cat,
this pawing furore, vertiginous spitting,
cats here then there, then not here and not there,
a hair's breadth between them and their skeleton love.

Tails, bones, chair, paw, they are spinning and the picture is
spinning, as they hiss in their fit, little beasts,
wild for the flesh of it, leaping in tempera strokes,
implacable button-blue eyes driven so strong
they could lick the egg-yolk from the paint they're made from.

Midtown Analysis

after Lorca's 'A Poet in New York'

Some of those edge-of-the-precipice
people are circling

smiling at breasts
asking directions to places of worship.

Sunlight glares through gaps in metal towers.
You are always walking

towards the Norman Foster building.
Men rise again

from a hole in the street.
A red hand flashes.

You reach for a cocktail
swallow a cab.

The Stock Exchange is not yet
covered in moss

but everyone's timing is off.
The sense of scale is mortifying.

A man wants to explore your bag/
your heart/your mind.

You lie upside down on his couch.
Vermont Clothbound Cheddar fills your throat.

He blames the axial
pull of the vertical.

You choke. He suggests
you try to be less literal.

This Is Not A Fad

Because I think you'd like me better as an artefact
I sit for ages in the sculpture park.
Flies settle on my arms.

Because I think you'd keep me close if I'd been customised
in a foundry, I will myself to turn to bronze.
Rain falls.

J'ai la verticale
dans mon esprit, I tell my spine,
channelling Matisse.

This is *not* a fad, like the long weekend I spent
being Danish in monochrome knitwear,
saying *tak* in exchange for tea,

this is for real. I shall remain here,
unmoved by sheep and hedge-trimmers,
until you notice me.

Niall

i.m. Niall McCabe

In the space between two worlds
I poach an egg. It's early.
I have fasted all night, a long night,
spent mainly talking with my spirit guide,
or rather, listening.
And when I say spirit guide, I mean
Niall, the Omagh boy from Drama School,
who used to be all thunder in the pub.

He wore his cloud-mass like a crown,
daring you to come and try and break it,
but in the dream, if he was weather,
he was a Gulf Stream,
he was a golden O reciting Shakespeare
in a parlour-room with chintzy décor.

Once I was afraid to catch his eye during a love-scene,
but in the parlour-room we gazed and gazed.
No-one could look away.
Of course, I begged him, 'How do you do it, Niall?'
because, in truth, I was desperate for his secret,
I was parched for his charisma,
but I couldn't hear his answer.

Still it was enough to see him back again and shining
resplendent in that parlour room,
after his miserable December passing.

The Opposite of Confidential

Nobody questions the birds.
Their trills are never subject to inspection or
forced to satisfy requirements.

Light-boned libertarians
(the opposite of confidential)
they cannot keep it in.

You will not see them lining up in rows
reeling off content-approved medleys
to a committee of creatures who know

nothing of song and who
certainly don't have wings.

Alex Wong

In writing these poems, I appear to have been exercised especially by the difficulties of thinking straightforwardly, and the even greater difficulties of speaking straightforwardly. Most of them are concerned, therefore, with habits of embroidery and veiling. In the terms of artifice they recreate certain larger problems of irony, style, and poise: problems we continually encounter in areas of our lives not appointed to be artificial at all. Still, these 'difficulties' and 'problems' are not altogether cheerless. If they are sometimes painful and momentous, at other times they seem to form a basis for curiosity, fantasy, imaginative pleasures, even of the giddiest sort. So, with variable proportions, a combination of anxiety and happy contentment governs my treatment of sentimentalism and bad faith, of extravagance – and of all leanings towards the figurative. I hope the sense of fun and the sense of the serious interfere with each other productively and not detrimentally. Also I hope that the form of the verse is not only discernible, but audible.

Pietà

The emotion of the *pietà*
Is control:

Animal sensation present
In structures of the soul—
The signs arisen
Out of *framed* feeling, *edified* dolours.

Control of the facial musculature
And of the voice—isn't
That the beginning of culture?
Dignity follows;

The first accomplishment
Is *sangfroid*.

A Comic Situation

Each one of an affectionate couple may be willing, as we say, to die for the other, yet be unwilling to utter the agreeable word at the right moment; but if the wits were sufficiently quick for them to perceive that they are in a comic situation...
— Meredith, 'Essay on Comedy'

Though to the surface every quiet conveys
        A token of you, as the near
Is tenant always for the far;—
                That I should hear
The narrowing step, your key chirp at the door
Again, already, even before
My having missed the touch of opposing days.

If our real pleasure issued spry and spry
        In passionate leaflets—every night,
Every day a thousand more,
                As green, as bright;

To blush at last, when blood in us dies down—
      Not wither like spring's crest and crown,
But each leaf turning golden by and by,

And living out our vigour—would that be best?
      Glow of the green is much to ask.
But some few, of a mottled kind,
          That like the mask
Taken for Agamemnon's, may be found
      Later—a leaf of gold in the ground—
Real; to be mistaken; to be kissed;

A solid proxy for a fading face—
      And for another face that fades,
Whose kiss it knows (or will have known).
          One masquerades
Not for a hood against you, nor to be seen
      By you alone; but to get some green
Into the mottle, for a safer place.

Green communications run a risk
      I took before, by which I earned
The strong and level good I keep.
          And I have learned
To prize what dedicated failures win—
      But no new rhetoric wherein
To pose affection; no figures bright and brisk,

No steady sentence, no precise avowal
      To bring sedately what is meant
Up to the surface; all I have
          Is sudden assent;
Candour of silence, I hope; candour of touch.
      And, called upon for more—for such
Greenery as before—why do I growl

Some boring mundane thing, sooner than say
      A word you want, I mean, and both
Know—so well—the shading of?
          To tell the truth:

Because the burden buoyed upon the tone
      Consists; but every form I own
Calls for atonement after; heavy dray

Makes in the moment every opportune
      Delivery appointed, it may be;
The same load in a smoother carriage,
              At a higher fee,
Might leave a cleaner track; and so to mend
      The method of conveyance I intend
Most earnestly; but when the nice poltroon

Determines to proceed against his flaws
      (No faults to you, in this one case),
It turns to hermitic flight from this
           Or that disgrace;
And you see nothing of the mind at work,
      And cannot tell that in the dark
Dim shuttles come over each night, with loving saws
      And grand confessions freighted.
Periods roll, beside you, soon
           Calumniated;—
Which more effective than one classic clause?

Groundwater

Soldatenfriedhof,
Vladslo.
Grand Crucifixion with Saints,
Convento di San Marco, Florence.

Not the wide sea with its whales, but the poppied
Plain we hardly know is water.

Even the full soil, this firm ground,
Groans to an arch beneath our shoes
Like the face of a pie rising

With all those bodies bundled,
How many per square metre;
Lungs breathing down in the hard, thick earth
That weighs like water round the floating dead.

★

What things can punctuate a soul or sting
    The nervous pore, like spirits, more
Than a dimple, uneven moving of the mouth,
    The heavy pinkness around your eyes;

    The grieving saints
    Are not so moving
As you, their drapery never so involving
    As that heavy pinkness,
    That falling and folding.

★

Will a face float up before me when I am drowning
At last, if fate will have it, and my lungs
Fill up with your so mortal breath;—
Lifting limbs in unrelinquent waves
    From the surface, the mirror, landwards;—
Falling back to your more responsive waters,
Drowning shyly, deliberately, being
Drowned at last.
                        Like a kitten in the sink;
But one whose lives are really nine
And stronger with every expiation. I am
No quietist, want to enjoy,
To see from every angle, taste
The salt, show each snare
The hardness of irony,
The softness of compliance;
But no precautious piety, no waste.

I am still afraid
For in that faceless golden head
I see no eyes.

Her blonde hair, her back to me,
The face I cannot see, pressed
Hard against another breast.

The blackness she sees
Is not the blankness I see
In that faceless golden head.

★

What if the ground simmers up around our legs—
Will it take us in, the dead slide round about us
Again? the ones with bullets in their backs;
The ones who wandered down there by mistake,
            Making a cup of tea;
Or those who had to use the forbidden key?

And will they be just like their photographs?
Their faces will be closed against the waters.

And even supposing the water should come to be
Fresh and cool and clear, seem sweet to savour,
Still as I bend to drink, I shall only see better
The crayfish scuttling in the rocks, and lobsters
Trailing strands of your hair in their grey hands,
Their colder-blooded, colder-blooded claws.

An Exercise in Prose

Inches from my face, the elbow
Of a corpulent lady relaxed to a wrinkle
Under the hem of a short grey sleeve. But I thought

Of those big, pale, pinguid Amalfi lemons!
The points peeping from the folds—
Soft peaks, solid in sun and rain.

Continental comparisons!
England smells so different in the sunshine;
O, there's enough to keep me
From lascivious agitations—
Till the afternoon, at any rate.

Sometimes, for a moment, I think——
————————wouldn't it be nice…
Though, on the other hand, gratitude.

The sun shines, or it rains
(An even better smell);   casting around
For someone to thank,
I find only myself—
(Or you, Papagena!);

Query: is this why God made us
In his own image?

Between my face and the window,
The motes are passing in calm traffic
Like futuristic vehicles in Fritz Lang's *Metropolis*.

'Thou Art of Purer Eyes than to Behold Evil'

The days of puncture—dusk—the nights of puncture.
   Calamitous flop,
      interminable trickle…
Despair in fixity,
      desperation at juncture.
   Affliction of the steadfast and the fickle.

The world is such a different place for others.
   The greater sadness
      of becoming fat;
Tenebrous degradation
      of old mothers.
      And who takes great enough account of that?

Disparities

Pontormo's Deposition

Fill the space around with colour;—
Makes the matter forfeit duller,
   Heavy in the floating dyes.

What to fix upon: the woozy
Figures, tinted gold and rosy—
   Or the face with lidded eyes?

One in faded green, like rotting
Flesh; the liquid standing, clotting,
   Still within; the life extinct;

Then the nine—men, boys and women:
Sky, blood-orange, lime and lemon;
   Musical, and poised, and prinked—

Rhythms of the fairy-story,
Daylight from the clerestory;
    Or, passed pain. Whatever it be,

Miserere, miserere:
Give us latitude to spare a
    Throb for foreign sympathy.

Stabat Mater (Pergolesi)
Comes—unruffled, cool, and hazy
    Round the sense—to help condole;

Making ready (*pertransivit*);
Making ready to conceive it:
    Finding out some ready hole.

Contristatus—and the lesson
Isn't simply of 'compassion';
    There, inside the drapery,

Daggers through the soul are passing,
Horrors yoking and amassing:
    He supremely not like me.

Partita

1

Flashing lights on the black invisible water,
And not a sign of the feathery, dusty scum,
That night you slipped away, renouncing relics.

Out in the garden, like fat fowl, the horse-chestnuts
Watch. Bloom-bunches—grapes, spectral, aspiring—
Nod in the branches. Light escapes the house,

Lends them a little glow. And they, composed,
Repay without scruple, giving indifferent sanction.
And the trees are trees, nothing else; but, full of fact,

Supplied themselves to the joinery of that passage—
Took their parts, and borrowed some of yours;
Aloof, to its spell of parting lent their forms.

2

Both her feet felt cool; she felt
The quick, hot heart-beat pressing down.

The mouth pulls in   to touch and mix,
And the eyes pull out, to watch—
        Trying to fix
              The unsurviving view,
To find assúrance of yóu. Isn't our demand
        To see ourselves
A will in each   to see someone else?

              3

    And I'd like
        To have heard
(No—I would
        Have liked to hear—?)
    Another word;
Though now it could
        Not bring you near.

Something remains.
    If I could swallow
All of it,   all of it;—
        Not as once,

When the one, in tangent bounds, made to engulf
        The other, foreign
        Matching form
Of self;

But now, because there *is* no chance;
Because your insubstantial strangeness
Makes no assertion now
              ——Do you follow?

Explanation. I call to witness
  A writer
  On matters
Spiritual and aesthetic,
  Inclined to fatness:

The love of anything
  (In a way)
Is a will to get all round it:
  That's to say,
To EAT it——
(Though the effect were emetic).

When kitty bites down on the wriggling mouse
  Really, she's only getting to know it.

The cat that swallows the lifeless bird
Does it because there's nothing else to be done with it,
To pút awáy, when shé can have nó more fún with it,
  The bulk of disappointment,

The autonomy failed she flirted with too hard.

So a thing remains:
  If I could swallow
All of it, all of it,
  Once for good——

And now, because there is no chance,
Because your wholeness drifts away,
Makes no assertions any more;
Because you are gone, and memory's poor,

Do I look to whom it may concern,
    Workers in shape
    And shape's revealers,
To furnish something new to learn?

Something to follow   decomposition
    Of a spooky trace
    Of a certain love—
A thing with a mojo to invite,
A mean discretion
        To unite.
                        Come, Leporello.

The Landowner

Rambler, direct your care
    To this magnificent gift.
Dare, rambler, to make durable those views.

——More trust, more debit.——
Lest the day come to see all trust is up,
Learn to speak newly over nature; build
Fresh castles for your chances to enjoy.
    Make chiffchaffs pay to find a way
Within, from a world not edified since Eden.

Hear in the song not only expressive bird,
But a history in your tongue, to beat the bounds.
As a child skims the ways of ideal gardens,
    So can you then,   so have you those
Adventures to go on with, grounds
Possible to their keepers;—outworks, follies.

The Disappointment

Asclepiadics

Crates, prised open and left, empty and splintery,
Lie slant over the curb, lit by a conical
Reach of yellow the rain's steady obliquity
Catches,   glinting its grain,   tilting.

                                        The sediment
Failure throws in the night's pitiful homecoming—
That dark silt, with its glint—sticks in the gullet and
Clogs. Night dredges the pool. Morning is rancorous.

Smell of fish by the drains;   yesterday, market day,
Fresh clear ice, and the sole, turbot and halibut;
     Lobsters, prawns; and the bright   herring, recumbent and
Slick.

       The butcher was here, poured in the gutter his
Pails of water, made red; tainted the cobblestones,
Daubed invisibly: sweet, cloying remembrances.

Bottles left on a wall, tattered umbrellas, a
Pair of shoes in the street, filling with rainwater:
Girls' flat pumps, set apart——four or five paces. He

Treads
    the pulp
       of a grey

                   newspaper; fingers the

Keys
    and phone
       in the damp

               pockets. (A paperclip…)

       Shadow sweeping the road,
rounding the walker each
             Space between the tall poles,

buzzing with energy.

Tall white spire!   *Camarade!*   Lonely pyramidal
Form! I make my approach. Gables occlude you, but
No thin brick barricades baffle your paladin!
One more corner to turn—pattering lambency—
Then:

      Declamatory stone, listen. My grievances
Beg derision. A poor, stammering Ganymede—
Bleached by light that returns, broad and phlegmatic, from
That scored plate of your face—shivers and kneels to you.
Give me decorous scorn.   Flesh is immovable.

Bagatelle in Spring

Very subtle seem the Spring's
      Achievements to the eye; and not
            Distent, as later, when the fruit
Is spent;—but to the brain, this crescent life
Weighs quite a lot, with all these little things.

It is like this. Something sings——
      The measure I don't follow; so many
            Nouns; what else? I cannot parse
The period: sticky leaf, and tiny coot,
And milky blossoms of the open-arse.

Lozenges against the grass,
      Where the banks slope to the waters:
            Bright quenelles of raw meringue,
Stowing their heads, each one, beneath a wing.
So neat;—but all those furry sons and daughters!

In my little *hortus*
    Conclusus, the soil produces
        Broods of pointed little red
Tulips, gaping—chick-like—to be fed.
They gape still, when a bee comes for the juices.

Another one chooses
    To rifle the public daffodils. Humming fills
        The horn: the voice is found
For its empty shouting. To its empty shouting
Only the pollinating bee gives sound.

On the public ground
    Are many daisies. I understand
        Better the meaning of
Their night-time looks, when candour scrunches close;—
Close, like fingers of a sprinkling hand.

About to land,
    The mallard returning to the park
        Curls in his body, like a prawn.
The wide horse-chestnut sweeps the lawn
Like a girl's fringe. It is getting dark.

        Yes——to the torture-mark
Patterning of the path;—the cracks of the bark;
And the craquelure of the dirt at the edge of the field,
    Ill-annealed.

Clunk

By the side of the road there came a flattish sense
Of something too familiar—with a clunk,
Like heavy doors on classic Cadillacs.
Was there charlatanry in my confession?

The highland cow, sitting beside the fence,
A silent but a sedulous quidnunc,
Encumbered in her melancholy locks,
Was shaggy and sad as Alfred Tennyson.

Like a fanfare of silver harpsichords
The moon was in full cry on the black woods
And rang metallic round our haloed pates.

Confected moments in heraldic state
Stood, romantic and rigid, like tapestry birds,
Among the wet lamps. They fly away, now, backwards.

Sufficient Honesty

Contradiction is a fact;—it mines
    Deep into the earth;—you cannot tunnel
        Under it;—its roots anticipate.

Its architecture fumbles to the light
    Whichever way you wander, and its spores
        Pursue you when you take the higher way.

Have commerce with your own hypocrisy.
    Know it. Remember every furtive face,
        And make a treaty with the colonies.

Duncan Montgomery

In its ratio of effort expended to goods produced, the search for genuine insight in writing can be like panning for gold: so much time and effort spent flailing, so many struggles with pyrite. I stuck at it mainly because of intellectual stubbornness. For now I find it helpful to think of each poem either as a research project (in the academic sense) or a gift.

My poem of the 'Three Dead Kings' is an arrant rewriting of 'De Tribus Regibus Mortuis', an alliterative poem whose sole manuscript witness is Bodleian Library, MS. Douce 302. This manuscript is the book of the blind fifteenth-century Shropshire priest John Audelay (d. 1426?), though his authorship of the poem is doubtful. Advocacy for an obscure text was among my primary motivations, and I'd direct interested readers towards Thorlac Turville-Petre's edition of the poem in his *Alliterative Poetry of the Later Middle Ages: An Anthology* (1989).

Three Dead Kings

At first only grunts, and hoof thuds heavy as horses',
over the hill that was silver
with the peeled paper bark of its birches

came a boar-shaped sound
which grew to an actual animal:
calm, bough-dappled darkness; a heart

magnetically thumping in a cubbyhole
as shouts and sennets took on flesh and metal.
In that hollow a hounded animal ended

surrounded by gillies and dog squabbles
with punctured sides and cobbled hooves
pegged out, back to the earth,

and with the barrel-chested look
of never having had to leave their lands
the three lords left.

★

The three lords left
and trotted home thinking of other things
as mist rose from the turf and swallowed their servants.

I was left stumbling
in the knee-deep mulch,
blind, with no ally or alibi.

The hills around looked like a landscape painted
at the palette's end, the acrid bright compounds
blurred into the pH-neutral dun of distant mountains.
As I faded into the background,
they howled at the murk, and afterwards told me
that the air cleared and they found themselves
riding through a caricature of bounty.

A pin-up glade
of light and sore-necked corn.

*

Their cheering stopped.
Out of the dark coppice,
shapes distinctly less than
men but more than skeletons slipped,
highwaymen with patterns
on their grave-clothes
like the three lords' flags.

The lords tugged on their bridles.
Their horses heaved
but like mechanical bulls:
plugged, earthed, static.
Checking their exits,
they babbled their faith
in Christ their saviour their merciful lord
but not even really in sentences.

They crossed themselves, cutting the corners.

*

They crossed themselves, cutting the corners.
None could plumb the blackness
of his father's eyes; no light,
no love bounced back.

'Hush, you remember the whole concerto:
me in the bed, the family gathered round.
The last rasp of the slab
like porcelain on porcelain,
uncritical obits poised for the evening chronicles.

Promised more pomp than the lid of a cistern,
promised massive marble, unbreakable choristers,
I lay there,

conscience a-quiver like a headless snake,
a mumble to fuddle grammarians.

Imperatives, defunct in present perfect,
said have said, have given freely, taken pains,
have kept your vows. Now, wherever your wife
waits, maudlin and downtrodden,
kneel there praying to your pissed-off God.'

★

Some say a miraculous
return to God can act
as evidence

only for the already-devout.

The three lords stacked
stone on stone
until a minster.

Always there are those who doubt.

★

Always there are those who doubt.
In the shallowing light their valley shut
like a moral tome with the lesson learnt.
The red sun soldered down into the hills.

Their wives were cherished, their baffled reeves
had to forget their practised meanness.
To deal with masons, glaziers, priests
flitting round chapels and almshouses.

And though these men were tasselled and clarioned
anyone can profit from their tale:
for who, blessed with the power of reason,
could hear their fate and not conclude
that God had had something to do with it?

The glazier's boy waits numbly with a bucket.
Workmen are plugging the sky-blue gaps
in a praying knight's armour with tar-paper;
are coming, armed with clippers and callipers,
to the north-west transept to gently
behead a line of pale-faced prelates.

Later, the boy sees silhouette-black
blur at its edges, fags floating on the scaffold.
The smithereened prophets are to be kept
underground in numbered boxes – five, six,
ten years, more, and dug up unwithered.

The Tax Advisor Is Only Thinking of Your Children's Children

The hourglass, lacking mechanical motion
or any part that needs to be oiled and up-kept
to stave off its eventual deterioration,
cannot be defined as a Wasting Asset.
It is subject to normal taxation
on capital gains. But that is not the real reason
the man with a forest of long-case clocks avoids it.

Nor its improbable waist, its frugal corset.
She is long-gone, though dearly beloved
and sorely, bitterly missed. It reminds him instead
of his wasting nature: clocks of mahogany,
walnut or oak, with birds of paradise limned
in the spandrels – brass hands counting on,
not down – will count for very little in the end

without informed wealth management and succession
planning. You've done so much right so far, collecting
racehorses, yachts, heavy machinery, fine wine,
all those assets of a limited lifespan
excluded from tax on the grounds that they can be
'exhausted by use or effluxion of time'.
But commonplace things obscure the bottom line.

Winter Sonnet

Now shadows have lengthened and sun
strikes our faces at such a sharp angle
burnt eyes can't make out the western
land in the afternoon, east in the morning

Fraying string, knotted round the handle,
stays the hinges of the door, and in the wind
the lean-to at the valley's head
knocks against its older harder neighbour

This the house, which like a dry-stone wall
turns to its advantage weight, a shoulder,
rusticated quoin-stones stacked
and squared against the squall that lifts away

The spiders' provisional scaffolding, too small
for eyes like ours to tell if they were hopeful

On a 'Calendar of Northern Landscapes'

Try to look at it like this: a landscape is not
a valley but a singularity, a locked dot
given that headspace can't be shared – our
great misfortune! – given pointing out a farm
can take as long as pointing out a star,
as I level my gaze down your outstretched arm
as an archer his down the shaft of an arrow.
Those hills are on your doorstep; have they ever
shone like that for you? Even if you'd been there
with your widest-angle eyes to catch the glow,
wind buffers landscape into frames, and cloud-cover
sieves the sun unevenly over the surface.
You'll find, once you've taken the camera's place,
the lake has dulled to steel. The fields are bare.

Headspace Shared

She thinks obscure thoughts, wants, itches beyond
omniscient narration. He's thinking
thoughts that only show up as a shadow
on a back-lit curtain, as the slimmest inklings
squeeze each way through the gasps and staccato commands.
Afterwards they stand, pink and peach, in the window;
she thinks someone's dropped a red cardigan
in a puddle and just left it for dead.
But it's a fox: the rusty flanks and head,
the brown brush and muddled undercarriage.
Willing to bet, we find, dust down and uncap
binoculars. We take a barrel each,
so our sight-lines agree on the jumper, the fox.
A red pheasant wobbles on a brown hen's back.

Knotting

I came into her room and she was still
plaiting her hair by the open window,
just inches from the pigeons on the sill.
Her mind had slipped from head-height, not

into the safety of the middle distance
we contemplate, unbuttoning a shirt
and standing in the nakedness of thought;
it brooded on her hands, her fingers knotting.

Knotting: we should more often use that word,
those minutes when the cooped-up mind
eludes its small circumference till we rise
apart again. The pigeons leapt their perch

to settle lower; her mind strayed, resting there,
alighting on her fingers, in her hair.

Brandon Courtney

My aim as a poet is to express – as clearly, simply, and succinctly as possible – the human experience: grief, recovery, hope, and despair. I don't consider my work imaginative, and I don't strive to create new images or complicated narratives. Rather, my work attempts to show the reader a moment, an idea, or some 'universal truth' in its fullest form. My poetry, though decidedly narrative, is not structured chronologically. I've often thought of my process as a kind of Feynman integral path, where each potential narrative course is cognitively calculated and discarded, until the poem takes its final shape. Reality, in plain language, is paramount in my work and, as such, it progresses through metre and rhyme, through human breath, repetition, and embodiment. The most successful of these poems are the ones that are accessible to anyone who reads them.

Beforelife

My mother found me
asleep in an abandoned skiff,
just one among hundreds
in a boneyard
of boats; I, just one boy
among thousands,
all sleeping.

In one boat lay my unborn
brother. In another, miscarriage,
water rising
through wooden floorboards.

And there, a blackbird
with a viper in its talons.
And there, a girl standing—
white as the flesh of an apple—
arms outstretched
measuring the rain.

My mother swam between boats
and lifted herself
on the gunwales, peering
into hollow keels
as if they were cribs, until she chose

me, a coral snake
poisonous and docile,
a body ringed in red and gold,
the poison she needed, the poison
she chose.

Shore Leave, Crete, 2002

We're standing
at the mouth
of the port, watching
mast lights
          sway on waves,

lean tenderly
into darkness.
In the ocean's deepest
gorge it takes a ship
          hours to sink

before it reaches the ocean floor;
it lists back and forth
          through water

like a leaf knocked
from its branch—
the only thing on earth

that takes that long
to fall. In the background,
the summit of Mt. Psiloritis
curves like a field

knife's blade,
and the naked eye
can't tell where the peaks end,
where sky begins.

Here, the seafront suffers:
green paint cut away
from chapel shutters
by sea salt and weather.

I don't believe
the wind blowing
through the campanile

is enough to move
the hammer
of the cassock bell,
clap the iron cup,

that the sound alone
is enough to bring men
to God, flesh and all.

You keep leading me
to ships, she says,
you keep leading me to ships.

Public Lashing, Iraq, 2004

Two men with no less thirst,
no less need for lust, kneel,
dishonored, the sand under
their knees ignorant to a body
bent in prayer—a coin of
breath kissed into the
offering plate of his chest—
or punishment. A dozen
lashes, each labial gash a
hymnal of sin, their shoulders
memorizing the shape of the
cleric's cane. How, a year in
Iraq, are your teeth—the
bruises sucked to the surface
of my neck the only proof I
have of war. You will never
hone the knife of your tongue
sharp enough to kill, sharp
enough to leave your mark on
my thighs. Tonight, on the
banks of the Tigris, you pour

an hourglass' worth of sand
from your boots, spin your
wedding ring before
pocketing it, as if the dead—
your wife—were looking
down into the black water of
our bodies, watching from
the trellis of heaven's bridge.
What are you waiting for?
The night is never dark
enough for our bodies to
hide; the night is never dark
enough to sleep.

Darwin's Narcissus

What about the nights
you stood in front
of Caravaggio's

painting and studied
Narcissus in bloom,
sure that his mouth,
        reflected

in a rippleless pool,
would meet water
and shatter his

reflection with a kiss?
Did you think of Annie,
running a comb

through your hair
just days before her
final fever?

         Above her
      convalescence bed,
      your face was the heaven

      she entered. And you
      buoyed over an image
      of yourself: her mouth,

      like yours, anchored
      into a pout,
      the sickled curve

      of her jaw, a lash of hair
      around her throat,
      every bone a bone
      you'd gifted her.

The Fear Muscles

1

Darwin's words resurface days after I've abandoned
his book—when our minds are much affected,

so are the movements of our bodies. Just days stateside,
rummaging rifles, ammunition, antique pistols

in the hotel's grand pavilion, I watch a boy level
the barrel of a Winchester at his younger brother's

chest—scarcely able to steady the carbide's weight.
Still, he must understand how delicately his brother

is tethered to this world. He shields his face
with both hands outstretched, turns away, flinching,

the body's only argument for life. He falls the way
he thinks soldiers fall, his palms clotting the phantom

---

wound, star-shaped, his slow plummet more crouch
than buckle, the hotel's floral carpet softly breaking

his body's momentum. I want to say no, a bullet
makes a man precisely aware of his body, aware

of the dusty Fallujah street—the vendors selling dried figs,
a chip of light glinting from razor wire, aware of shots

fired during a wedding party, and those fired by a sniper.
But how does the boy know to keep his eyes closed, to lie

motionless, holding his breath? Does he know
when the game is over? How does he know when to rise?

II

In Basra, I steal away to the burnout latrine, a Glock
holstered in my belt. I press blue steel to my mouth's

soft palate, bite down hard into the barrel, roll its metal
like the Eucharist on my tongue. I think of nothing;

I fall asleep, wake only when the gun slips from my hand.
Now, I swallow two teardrop pills to sleep, dream

a prescription dream. Most nights I pull the trigger,
jerk awake to sounds my mind mistakes for the bullet's

sudden punch: shutters slapped against our pane, my lover's
hair brushed against my temple. Tomorrow, she'll tell

me of a soldier's wife found shot in the back
seat of her minivan, a duct tape gag wreathing her head.

Prayer

Forgive me the man, his flesh
    taken up and beaten
breathless on Arabian waves;

the swells' grey refrain
    has never left
my tongue. Each night
he dies and becomes one breath
    inside the prophet.

Forgive, if it is possible,
    the slush of stars low
above Baghdad,
brighter than flames
men start in sockets of sand.

Forgive the clay, soil, dust,
marble, anything that holds
the blast pattern's shape,
    the Tomahawk's echo,

louder than the detonation
    from which it's borne;

soldiers who sink,
stock–still, into the bomb's
    cindered hole,

who bed down with a camel's
    saddle blanket,
stinking of smoke, blood,
sandalwood.
    I know you cannot

forgive me the voice
    that was once
in his mouth, my hands
that have yet to hold
    my son.

      I know you cannot
forgive my fingers, so I ask
    that they may break,
finally, after all they did.

The Grief Muscles

  Darwin calls it universal,
        himself witness to an Indian elephant
weeping, captured and bound in Ceylon,

stock still, tears the size of pisco grapes
      the only indication of her suffering. Grief,
    he wrote after speaking to a mother
about her dying son, was an orchestra

of contracting facial muscles: pleated furrows, eyes pinched,
        abrupt arch of her brows, a relief
sculpture, levo—to rise from the surface.

        How easily I think of the woman
and her sickly son, Darwin, the mewling elephant,

    remembering me with you:

      ten years too young to marry, to own anything
worth owning, a farm

    that needed a new foundation and roof. I should have left

it to the fields to swallow whole; I didn't

know it at the time, but you took
                                    a dozen rolls of film
our first summer, documenting my slow progress:

              wedging rotten siding from the façade with a claw hammer,
running blood-colored rust from the pipes, patching

the chimney's fissures with mortar. Bats, you thought,
entered through the eyelets and circled pell-mell

above our bed while we slept, feasting on a fog of mosquitoes,
moths drawn to the warm light of the lampshade. And me, five years away

              from temperance, sobriety,
muscled into your photo with its smear of backdrop leaves, bottled bourbon
   cocooned in glass, your camera trained on the furnace stack,

              my gaunt face:
the orbicular, corrugators, and pyramidal muscles
                                    quaked
with regret, which Darwin wrote is indistinguishable from sorrow.

Sinsemilla

for Jason Courtney

The last time I saw my brother
alive—skinny, sleepless
          in the aluminum kiln

of his singlewide, stringing,
restringing our father's guitar—
          he spoke soberly

about the drift of his rig.
He thought, often, of crossing
the highway's centerline,

the 18-wheeler's grill
hammering the guardrail.
    He looks like my father,

decades earlier, liquored
on bottom-shelf bourbon,
not yet washed into the darkest

harbor of our mother.
No, this night we both wait
for the branch of our father

to bear any fruit.
He drops the needle
on the pupil of a black record—

slow country, Delta blues—
    rolls another joint
of Sinsemilla, seedless,

in the linoleum-bright kitchen,
then finger picks,
fumbles through chords,

lyrics, the silver minnow
of his tongue flashing
    inside his dark mouth.

from Hold Fast

18

Tonight, I'll tell her anything she needs
to hear: Yes, the heart, like a bone, can break

more than once. Yes, my mother cried
when I called to tell her I was going to war;

my father shook my hand, told me
only heroes come home horizontally.

Yes, I can speak Arabic: rifle, bandage,
kneel. Yes, I've been shot; the bullet

is still inside me, swimming slowly
toward my heart. Yes, there's more blood

inside a man than light inside the sun.
Yes, my best friend drowned; I have

the latitude and longitude tattooed above
my heart. No, you can't touch it.

Yes, I've swallowed the Euphrates.
I've tasted salt from the Arabian Gulf,

which for a week, was another man's
grave. Yes, I drank it in.

19

Three months into deployment,
Dyer refuses to shower.

When Doc tells him a lack of hygiene
is the first sign of mental illness,

he doesn't listen. We arm ourselves
with bottles of bleach, wire brushes,

Brillo pads, pull him from his coffin-
rack, muscle him into a shower stall.

We scrub the filth from his fingers,
scour his skin with Clorox.

After, bleeding, his back and chest
look like the surface of a frozen lake,

a hundred small blades of skates
cutting circles—recklessly,

pointlessly—in the ice.

20

My father says the war changed me
from a killer to a pacifist; I refuse

to fillet the fish he pulls from the lake.
I refuse to slip the blade between gills,

fold back their pearlescent scales,
cut away what little meat their bodies

offer. As children, my brother and I
would wander the woods behind

our house, shooting anything that startled.
We killed to kill, sometimes to maim,

never to keep or cook. I can't take
my eyes away, now, as my father opens

fish after fish on old newsprint
in the garage. I close my eyes

when something like darkness eats
into their translucent hearts.

Bodega

I

The last time I stood this close to an Iraqi,
I was inside the skin
of a Kuwaiti ship off the coast
of Al-Ahmadi, zip-tying a man's ankles

to the metal legs of a chair, my pistol aimed
at the bluest vein
in his throat, safety off, finger on
the trigger. Now, we're standing across

from each other, close as two wrists
cinched in prayer,
only a glass counter to separate us.
Every morning, I purchase

the same things: black coffee, cigarettes.
Every morning he says:
Are you trying to kill yourself? I say nothing.
He laughs.

II

The graffiti's long been scrubbed
from the bodega's brick façade,

yet a ghost of spray-painted letters
remain: *Haji, Towel-head.*

Someone's shot a hole into the pane
glass—it sounds like a sucking

chest wound whenever the wind
hits the window.

III

From under the counter, he pulls
a long black rifle, new, never fired.

He says it's for protection; *hold it,*
he says, *pretend I'm your worst enemy.*

IV

He wouldn't forgive me if I told him,
so I don't. I don't tell him how the hand

that's held a rifle remembers its weight
or how, years ago, I watched three Iraqis

drown in the Arabian Gulf. I want to tell
him how I tried to save them all, held

one man's head above the whitecaps,
our mouths close enough to kiss.

He wouldn't forgive me if I did, so I don't.

V

In the morning, his young son kneels,
scours fresh spray paint from the storefront's

brick wall: *Terrorists.* He's started at the end,
managed to erase all but the word *Terror.*

I roll my sleeves to my wrists,
cover the tattoo that means *Death
Before Dishonor.*

Post-Traumatic Stress Disorder

In a country you'll never see,
an IED tears apart a man.
He tries again and again

to stand on legs no longer
there, the lesser knots
of his knees finally untied.

In cities built on sand,
the scar carries the wound
into the future; the bandages
won't stop unraveling.

Sometimes, blood, like breast
milk, leaves the body
through the smallest of holes.

No, there is nothing
miraculous about the body—
it ends. I've stood this close
to violence; I'll never be the same.

John Clegg

I'm all for an approach to reading poetry that treats it as a concentrated version of ordinary speech; that presupposes an intent to communicate; that brings in any context or outside information which feels valuable at the time; that takes note of first response, which may give a better sense of tone than rereadings; that defers, perhaps indefinitely, theoretical questions, until we can be satisfied we've apprehended the poem somewhat on its own terms; that is prepared to quibble and argue with the poem or poet, and does not over-scrupulously resist identification between the two. I suppose these principles inform the way I write as well, but I don't want to probe too closely – or rather, I suspect that any attempt to do so would involve such a degree of post-hoc reconstruction and falsification that it would end up no better than anyone else's informed guess. You tell me.

Lacklight

At first we didn't call the dark 'the dark';
we saw it as a kind of ersatz light,
a soupy substitute which shucked the hems
and wrinkles from our objects. That was nice.

And later on we came to love the dark
for what it really was – admired how
(unlike a candle) it could fill a room,
(unlike a torch) it focused everywhere,

(unlike a streetlight) it undid the moths,
(unlike a porchlight) anywhere was home,
(unlike a star) it couldn't be our scale.
In utter darkness we were halfway down.

Then came the age of lacklight, loss of measure,
darkness turned inside to cast a darkness
on itself. Though 'age' would make it finite.
Perhaps we're stuck there, straining in the lacklight.

Still, across the last however long,
I've noticed something budding, vaguely sensed
a nerve untie and reconnect itself.
I think my lacklight eye is almost open.

The Lasso

That I had time to think, *I still have time*
not to correct my grip but drop the rope
before the lasso fell and yanked away
the loop I'd somehow nocked around my thumb.

That I had time to notice I could think
and that the time to think in was reserved
for thought, like hours in a monastery.
I knew, because I saw and still held on.

That I had time, time sinking like the rope
around the moment's neck, and I had thought
like slackness in the rope, the little loop
that half a moment's tension would wrench true.

That I had time and then the time was taut.
My thumb, erratic firework, shot past,
and in the time reserved for me to breathe
I swear my wrung hand tightened on the rope.

The Signal and the Noise

Frostbite starts
as numb song from the palm,
the lowest note left thrumming in a bellrope.

By the time
it reaches the attention
fingertips have swum outside your orbit.

Antsy void
where every sense but vision's
blared with signal: in the white, distractions

amplify
and newfound fistlessness
is one more datum. You lose purchase

on the edges
of your focus first. Then
one by one the other outposts blink blank.

The Great Tradition

I followed every wire in the server room
once, waiting for the photocopier-
cum-scanner to flog through another
thousand pages, hitchless, you could
hear the all-clear subsong. My job
was to stand in that cool air and unjam
stuck sheets. This was Cambridge
and the server room was former King's
accommodation, reaching through
the racks your hand brushed marble
sunflower bosses on the fireplace,
I pinched the inside wire, keeping track
and thought of Heather, could her book
be really on *The British-Irish Lyric*
as a whole or was I misremembering?
Two wires seemed to have no terminus.

Roadkill Ocelot

Hard to imagine
sleek except where she's
been drawn back
to the sleek bone.

Scuzzy, says the daughter
of the man who stopped
to see what we
were standing round.

It fits the mottle:
working camo
scuzzying her outline
must have been what killed her.

Microbiome
of the blown gut
shimmers, overblooming
on the tarmac.

Her expression
fluctuates, depending
on the angle
which you read it from.

The narrowest surprise
conceivable
shades into (are you
sure?) this sudden, massive joy.

Tenaya Overwintered in Yosemite

Acorns under earth a year
leach bitterness and blacken,
go well raw or roasted.

Our hotel
resorts to Davy lamps.
The bar taps and the TVs stop.

Ground acorns steep in boiled water.
This is changed each day.
They're edible when it runs clear.

The snow is doorframe deep.
All loans of snowshoes, snow shovels and skis
require a credit card deposit.

Acorn bread is wrapped in amole leaf
then placed among
an 'oven' of hot stones.

All vehicles without tyre chains
will not be towed.
You must return for them in spring.

Rain Bird

When the screw thread on a plastic nozzle head
gives way, which come to think of it's
their only failure mode, I mosey over
with a satchel of replacement nozzle heads,
a square-bit key to turn the intermittent off,
a while spare to dawdle vaguely shaded, like the beans, by spritz.

The rain-bird is a sort of square-bit key
unlocking California to green.
You think about the Calaveras
crumpling behind the dam, extruded
through its pinchpoints, culverts, aqueducts
to hammer here, a thousand wings in sync, down mile latitudes.

Yessir, you think about it for a while,
wing as waterfern, as fern of water,
wing as feather, fractalling to spray
to swansdown drifting through no breeze
to gloss on leaf, the green blade of the possible.
Then you jerk the key back and start for the access road.

Ramsonde

Every morning with his ramsonde and resistograph
he plots the snowpack's weakness as a jaggy coastline.
From that gauges chance of avalanche.

Within his quadrant he can radio roads closed,
bar skiers from the slopes, and snowshoed hikers
dawdle over coffee for his estimate.

His rifle is dismantled, reassembled, constantly.
His map too, and his sense of how the snowfalls
slot together, layer into layer.

Once, along the ridge, he felt the ground writhe
underneath his boots, and then the mountain shrugged.
He crawled out downslope, dragging home his leg.

Unchoosy about company: the bear man following
a collar's radar blip to find the den, the helicopter
ambulance he'll chat conditions with.

Responsibility is hammering the ramsonde, milled
harpoon, into the glacier's whaleback, to listen
for the sigh. The sigh flows upward through his hand.

Holy Toledo

Was it *somewhere near Salinas* Kris let Bobby
slip away, or *somewhere miscellaneous*?

Oxford '61, say – Kris watched Auden lecture,
boxed for Merton, carpooled with the young Morse.

On the train to Carmen's party, A. explained
why *undead* was an oxymoron.

*I pulled my harpoon out of my dirty red
bandanna* – was that Kris's word for *harp*

(harmonica) or *hypo*?
Not a trade name, though the first

harmonicas were marketed as *aeolians*.
Sing, breeze, blow it soft against the river –

as Auden bungs a notebook in the Cherwell,
as a frogman rises with the Saxon buckle,

as the punt squirms, Kris blinks, Bobby vanishes –
as Carmen butterflies into the Thames

off Port Meadow,
the smoulder finds the fringe of kindling

beneath our scrappy bbq, and kicks in
like the drums on 'Shipwrecked in the Eighties'.

T for Texas

Every source seems to take it as read
that in those days 'brakeman' was synonym
for 'agreeable', that his yodel mimicked, lyrebird-fashion,
a trainwhistle's dip and wheel, its Doppler
ripple through gaps in the rockwall –

though now it sounds more like a trick
of the wind down an empty canyon, plaintiveness
in his voice mistaken for plain good nature.
TB in German translates as 'addiction to dwindling'.
The next train does not call at this station.

Bloomsbury

G.S. Fraser grousing about Empson's voice,
'odd, sad, snarly, rising now and again
to a very high pitch, the Cambridge voice
of the 1920s' – Bloomsbury's run-out groove.

Ten minutes late for work, I listen
to a string quartet tune up in someone's
living room on Thornhaugh Street.
Nearby, the architecture bows and scrapes,

The University of London here
expresses its sincere regret for this extension,
undertaken without the permission or the knowledge
of the Russell Family, who at no stage were consulted –

When Woolf says that *human nature*
changed completely in December 1910
I distrust her, but maybe it changed twice.
The violin, sad, snarled, uncurls its Cambridge voice.

Donald Davie in Nashville

'However sparred or fierce
the furzy elements…' – the steel guitars
he never learnt to recognise,
Merle Haggard's voice, a bed of tinny
feedback – 'let them be but few,
and spaciously dispersed,
and excellence appears.'
His taxi to the airport
ups the volume on a gospel show.

A transplant, hating country music,
his new campus, how the students
see him as a pinko Brit
and not the brawling Tory of *PN Review*,
he takes a backward look at Music City –
neon bars, the empty megachurch. It's sparse as hell.

Peach Tree

for Jack Baker

Things grow around particularities,
a footpath doglegged at a field boundary,
a feral peach conniving with the angle
of a roof to funnel sunlight
through its leaves and pericarp.
Jack said that certain poems
could bend thought like that,
'The Auroras of Autumn' he mentioned.

We can be sure that no-one
reads a poem Rilke's way,
now change your life, bam,
now, presumably, change it again.
You'd never get through an anthology.
Really to read properly is to buzz low over
our future lives in a cropduster,
throwing out stumbling blocks.

Biographies

Authors

Nic Aubury was born in Watford in 1974 and grew up in the Midlands. He read Classics at Oxford and now teaches Latin and Greek for a living. He has had two books of poetry published by Nasty Little Press (*Small Talk*, 2011 and *Cold Soup*, 2013) and has performed his poetry at various festivals including Port Eliot, Latitude and the Cheltenham Poetry Festival. Poems of his have also appeared in Sophie Hannah's novel *The Carrier*, in the Penguin anthology *The Poetry of Sex*, and on BBC Radio 4's *Woman's Hour*.

Vahni Capildeo is a British Trinidadian writer of poetry and prose. Her recent books are *Utter* (Peepal Tree, 2013) and *Measures of Expatriation* (Carcanet, forthcoming 2016). In 2014 she was a judge for the Forward Prizes and the Small Axe Poetry Competition. She is co-creating new responses to Euripides' *Bacchae*.

John Clegg was born in Chester in 1986 and grew up in Cambridge. He studied for a PhD at Durham University. In 2013, he received an Eric Gregory Award. A pamphlet, *Captain Love and the Five Joaquins*, is published by Emma Press. He works as a bookseller in London.

Joey Connolly grew up in Sheffield and studied in Manchester. His poetry and criticism have appeared in magazines including *PN Review*, *Poetry Review*, *Warwick Review*, *Poetry Ireland Review* and various other reviews. He received an Eric Gregory award in 2012 and his first collection is forthcoming from Carcanet. He edits the poetry journal *Kaffeeklatsch*.

Brandon Courtney was born and raised in Iowa, served four years (1999–2003) in the United States Navy (Operation Enduring Freedom), received his BA in English from Drake University in 2010, and his MFA from Hollins University in 2012. He is working towards an advanced degree at the University of Chicago.

Adam Crothers was born in Belfast in 1984. He lives in Cambridge, where he completed a PhD in English at Girton College in 2010; he works as a library assistant, book reviewer and teacher.

Tom Docherty was born in Glasgow in 1989 and brought up in Hamilton. He studied for undergraduate and graduate degrees at the University of Glasgow before receiving an MPhil in Medieval and Renaissance Literature at the University of Cambridge. He has now started work there towards a doctorate, which is currently about the poetry of Geoffrey Hill.

Irish writer Caoilinn Hughes' first collection, *Gathering Evidence*, was published by Carcanet in 2014. Poems from the collection won the 2012 Patrick Kavanagh Award and other prizes. She recently moved from New Zealand (where she completed her PhD at Victoria University of Wellington) to the Netherlands, where she teaches at Maastricht University. She is currently writing her second poetry collection and a novel.

J. Kates lives in Fitzwilliam, New Hampshire.

Eric Langley is a lecturer in Shakespeare at University College London. In 2009, he published a book on suicide and narcissism in Shakespeare with Oxford University Press, and is currently writing on Renaissance notions of disease transmission and sympathy. His poetry has appeared in *PN Review*, and he previously worked on the editorial team of *Stand* magazine.

Nyla Matuk was born in Winnipeg in 1967 and now lives in Toronto. She holds an MA in English from McGill University and her first poetry collection, *Sumptuary Laws*, was published with Véhicule Press in 2012. She was shortlisted for the *Walrus* Poetry Prize and the Gerald Lampert Award, and her poems have appeared in *PN Review*, *Hazlitt*, *Best Canadian Poetry in English 2012*, *The Walrus*, *Maisonneuve*, *The Literary Review of Canada*, the *Best American Poetry* blog, and in several other journals and magazines.

Duncan Montgomery was born in the north-east of England in 1991. He read English at Trinity Hall, Cambridge, where he is now a graduate student with interests in print culture and historical writing in early modern England. He is especially interested in book illustration, as he is also a wood-engraver.

André Naffis-Sahely is a poet, critic and translator. His poetry was most recently featured in *Best British Poetry 2014*. Recent and forthcoming translations include *The Physiology of the Employee* by Honoré de Balzac (Wakefield Press, 2014), *The Confines of the Shadow, Vol. I* by Alessandro Spina (Darf Books, 2015) and *Selected Poems* by Abdellatif Laâbi (Carcanet Press, 2016).

Ben Rogers lives and works in London. He studied English at Cambridge and Cinema & TV Studies at the British Film Institute. His poems have appeared in publications including *Magma, 14, Succour* and *Long Poem Magazine*. A pamphlet is forthcoming from Emma Press.

Lesley Saunders has published five books of poetry and collaborated with artists, photographers, sculptors, dancers, and a composer and choir. Her most recent collection, *The Walls Have Angels*, was inspired by a residency at Acton Court, a hauntingly beautiful Tudor house, and its summer visitors in 1535, King Henry VIII and Anne Boleyn.

Claudine Toutoungi's poetry has appeared in various publications including *PN Review* and *Magma*. Her plays *Bit Part* and *Slipping* have been produced by the Stephen Joseph Theatre. She adapted *Slipping* for BBC Radio 4 in 2014. She is currently writing *Deliverers*, a new play for BBC Radio 4.

David Troupes grew up in Massachusetts, though he currently lives in West Yorkshire. He has published two books of poetry with Two Ravens Press, and his comic strip *Buttercup Festival* appears regularly in *PN Review*. He is pursuing a PhD at the University of Sheffield on Ted Hughes and Christianity.

Molly Vogel is a poet from Thousand Oaks, California. She has been shortlisted for the Jane Martin Poetry Prize and the Edwin Morgan Poetry Award. Her poems have appeared in *Fish, Aesthetica*, and *PN Review*. She is currently completing a PhD in Creative Writing at the University of Glasgow.

Rebecca Watts was born in Suffolk in 1983 and now lives in Cambridge, where she works in a library and as a freelance editor. In 2014 she was selected as one of the Poetry Trust's Aldeburgh Eight. She is working towards her first collection.

Judith Willson has worked as a teacher and in publishing. Her edition of selected poems by Charlotte Smith, and *Out of My Borrowed Books*, an anthology of work by three Victorian women poets, are published by Carcanet.

Alex Wong is a literary scholar living in Cambridge, where he has recently completed his doctoral studies. For Carcanet he has edited a selection of Swinburne's verse (2015).

Editors

Michael Schmidt is editorial and managing director of Carcanet Press which he founded with friends in 1969. He has also been the managing editor of *PN Review* since 1972. He is a literary historian, poet, novelist and translator, a Professor of Poetry, and a writer in residence at St John's College, Cambridge.

Helen Tookey lives in Liverpool, where she teaches creative writing at Liverpool John Moores University. Her first full-length collection of poetry, *Missel-Child*, was published by Carcanet in 2014; her other publications include *Anaïs Nin, Fictionality and Femininity* (Oxford University Press) and, co-edited with Bryan Biggs, *Malcolm Lowry: From the Mersey to the World* (Liverpool University Press).

Acknowledgements

Vahni Capildeo
'Inhuman Triumphs' was published in the *Cambridge Literary Review*.
'Pobrecillo Tam' was published in *Visual Verse*, after an image by Nick
Simpson. 'Slaughterer' and 'Stalker' were published in *PN Review*. 'Fire
& Darkness: And Also / No Join / Like' was published in *Poetry &
Audience*. 'Louise Bourgeois: Insomnia Drawings' was published in *Molly
Bloom*. 'Mercy and Estrangement' was commended in *Café Writers* Poetry
Competition 2012. 'The Prolongation of the Spine and the Stretched
Neck Approximate the French Philosopher Only to his Own, and Airy,
Beast' was published in *aglimpseof*.

John Clegg
'The Signal and the Noise' first appeared in *Magma*. 'Donald Davie in
Nashville' first appeared in *Poetry Review*.

Joey Connolly
'What You've Done', 'Your Room at Midnight was Suddenly' and
'Coming to Pass' first appeared in *PN Review*. 'A Brief Glosa' first appeared
in *Magma*. 'That Rogue Longing' first appeared in *Stand*. 'Poem in Which
Go I' first appeared in *Poems in Which*. 'The Finest Fire-Proofing We
Have' first appeared in *The Lifeboat*. 'Of Some Substance, Once' first
appeared in *Poetry Wales*. '[untititled]' and 'Themselves' first appeared in
Cadaverine.

Brandon Courtney
'Shore Leave, Crete, 2002' was first published in *Prick of the Spindle*. 'Public
Lashing, Iraq, 2004' was first published in *Thrush Poetry Journal*. 'The
Fear Muscles' was selected for inclusion in the anthology *Remembrances
of Wars Past: A War Veterans Anthology*, ed. Henry Tonn. 'Bodega' was
first published in *Tinderbox*. 'Beforelife' was first published in *Cream City
Review*. 'Sinsemilla' is forthcoming from the *Boston Review*. 'The Grief
Muscles' was first published in *Vinyl Poetry*. All the poems are included in
The Grief Muscles (Sheep Meadow Press, 2014).

Adam Crothers
'Blues for Kaki King' was first published in *PN Review*; 'The Bone Fire' in *Poetry Proper*; 'Dirge' in *Eborakon*; and 'Matthew' in *The Literateur*.

Tom Docherty
'Theory of Tuning Pianos', 'At the Grave of Ludwig Wittgenstein', and 'Centoum' have appeared in *PN Review*; 'The Herbs of Scotland' was first published in *Magma*.

Caoilinn Hughes
'We Are Experiencing Delay' was first published in *The Irish Times*. 'Airbowing in Second Violins' was one of a group of three poems that won the Cúirt New Writing Prize 2013. 'Communion Afternoon' was first published in *The Yellow Nib*. All the poems here except 'On Bringing the Common Cold to Tahiti' and 'Apple Falls From the Tree' were included in *Gathering Evidence* (Carcanet, 2014).

J. Kates
'Orientation' was published in *The Massachusetts Review*; 'Schein: A Toast' in *The Antioch Review*; 'The Ax-murderer's Daughter' in *Takahe* (New Zealand), in *The Prairie Star*, and in *The Briar Patch* (Hobblebush Press); 'Learning to Shoot' in *The Ledge*, and in *Metes and Bounds* (Accents Publishing); 'Out' in *Mid-American Review* and *The Briar Patch* (Hobblebush Press); 'The Uses of Poetry' in *Sulphur River Literary Review*; 'At Starfire Lake' in the anthology *Bread for this Hunger* (Crab Creek Press); 'Winterlied': in *PN Review*; 'Words' in *Cornucopia* (New Zealand) and in *Metes and Bounds* (Accents Publishing).

Eric Langley
'Glanced' and 'Tact' first appeared in *PN Review*.

Nyla Matuk
'Meditation After Seeing *Hannah Arendt*' and 'Aquatic Hermeneutics' both appeared in *PN Review*. 'Happenings on the Cover of the *New Yorker*' appeared in *The Fiddlehead*.

Duncan Montgomery
An earlier version of 'Three Dead Kings' was published in *PN Review*. '1939', 'Winter Sonnet' and 'Knotting' also appeared in *PN Review*.

André Naffis-Sahely
'A Summer Visit', 'The Carpet that Wouldn't Fly' and 'A Kind of Love' were featured in the *Days of Roses II* anthology. 'The Translator' appeared in *Poetry London*. 'Postcard from the Cape' appeared in *The Mimic Octopus*. 'Apparition' appeared in the *Australian Poetry Journal*.

Ben Rogers
'Sheherazade' was previously published in *Magma*; 'A Space Azalea' was previously published in the US journal *Transom*.

Lesley Saunders
'Indigo' was first published on the *Manchester Poetry Prize 2010* website. 'Olfactory' was first published in *Poetry London*. 'Army Musician' was first published in *Divers* (Aark Arts, 2008). 'Census' was first published in *Cloud Camera* (Two Rivers Press, 2012). 'Gaudete' was first published in *The Walls Have Angels* (Mulfran Press, 2014). 'Particulare Care' was first published in *Ordinary Treasure* (self-published pamphlet, 2012). 'Personajes: Poems after Remedios Varo' was first published in *PN Review*.

Claudine Toutoungi
'Without Moorings' was shortlisted for the Bridport Prize 2014. 'Midtown Analysis' was longlisted in the 2014 National Poetry Competition and published in *PN Review*. 'Niall' was published in *PN Review*. 'Winter Wolf' and 'Cats Breakfasting' were published in *Magma*. 'The Opposite of Confidential' was published in *Erbacce*.

David Troupes
'Swimming at Ovens Mouth' and 'Echo Lake' were published in *Earthlines*; 'Mount Pomeroy and Mount Liza' in *Entanglements*; 'And to Those Bleak Hills' in *The Clearing*; and 'The Allotments of Land Were Divided' in *Magma*.

Molly Vogel
'Danaë', 'Interruption and Completion of a Thought', 'Lessons on How to Understand a Famous Painting' and 'Glesga Prayer' were published in *PN Review*. 'Lessons on How to Understand a Famous Painting' was republished in the *Aesthetica* Creative Writing Annual, 2015. 'The Child Dreaming in a Poet's House' was highly commended and printed in the *Fish Poetry Prize Anthology*, 2014. A version of 'Isle of Skye' first appeared in 'The Written Image' exhibition, Scottish Poetry Library, November

2013. 'Isle of Skye' was republished in the *Edwin Morgan Poetry Award 2014* pamphlet.

Rebecca Watts
'Emmeline's Ascent' was first published in *Cycle Lifestyle*, and reprinted in *Einstein & the Art of Mindful Cycling* (Leaping Hare Press, 2012). 'Turning', 'Visitor', 'The Molecatcher's Warning' and 'German Tinder Box, c.1800' were published in *PN Review*. 'Two Bats' was published in *The North*. 'Letter from China' was published (in English and in German translation) in *Die Gazette*.

Judith Willson
'Noctilucent', 'James Turrell's *Deer Shelter Skyspace*, Yorkshire Sculpture Park', 'The years before', 'Watching a nineteenth-century film in the twenty-first century' and 'In the jagged months' were first published in *PN Review*.